Diana Goodey   Noel Goodey

Messages

Student's Book

1

CAMBRIDGE
UNIVERSITY PRESS

	Grammar	Vocabulary and Pronunciation	Listening and Reading skills	Communicative tasks
Module 1 Facts				
Unit 1 **What do you remember?**	• Revision: *I'm, I live, I've got* • He/She …, His/Her … • Classroom language • *Can*: asking for permission and help	• Revision of known vocabulary • Numbers and dates • The alphabet • Things in the classroom	• Punctuation • Listen to and understand a song • Read a letter in English • *Life and culture*: Alphabet world	• Tell the class about yourself • Ask and answer questions about you and your friends • Talk to your teacher in English • Write a letter to an English friend
Unit 2 **Are you ready?**	• *Be*: affirmative, negative, questions, short answers • Questions with *What, Where, Who, When* • Singular and plural nouns	• Members of a band • Interests and activities • Countries and cities • Geography • *Rhythm drill*: word stress	• Read an email • Listen to an interview for a student survey • Listen to a radio quiz • *Life and culture*: The UK	• Ask for and give information • Write about an imaginary band • Describe your interests • Talk about cities and countries • Play a quiz game
Review	*Study skills:* Your coursebook *How's it going?:* Progress check *Coursework:* Facts about me			
Module 2 Things and people				
Unit 3 **What have you got?**	• *Have got* • *A, an, some, any* • Possessive *'s* • Possessive adjectives • *This/these, that/those*	• Everyday things • Families • *Rhythm drill*: plural nouns: [s], [z], [ɪz]	• Listen for specific information • Read an announcement • *Story: The Silent Powers* Chapter 1 • *Life and culture*: Collections	• Talk about possessions, and things you use at school • Say who something belongs to • Write a description of a family
Unit 4 **Descriptions**	• *What is/are … like?* • *Has got* • Adjectives	• Appearance and personality • The body • *I've got a headache/cold* • [h] and links between words • Stress in sentences	• Read a 'Happiness Recipe' • Listen to personal descriptions • Listen to and understand a song • *Story: The Silent Powers* Chapter 2 • *Life and culture*: London	• Ask about and describe things • Write a 'Happiness recipe' • Describe people's appearance and personality • Say how you feel • Write about an imaginary person
Review	*Study skills:* Using a dictionary *How's it going?:* Progress check *Coursework:* Important things to me			
Module 3 Daily life				
Unit 5 **My world**	• Present simple: affirmative, negative, questions, short answers • Revision of question forms • *Wh-* questions	• Things you do regularly • Scary things • Verb + [s], [z], [ɪz] • Stress and intonation in questions	• Read about British teenagers • Listen to and understand a song • *Story: The Silent Powers* Chapter 3 • *Life and culture*: Schools	• Describe things you do • Write about teenagers • Talk about fears, likes and dislikes • Write a questionnaire • Make a conversation about daily life
Unit 6 **I'm usually late!**	• Present simple + frequency adverbs • *Have + a meal*, etc.	• Food, drink and meals • The time • Daily routines • *Rhythm drill*: vowel sounds	• Read and listen to a questionnaire • Listen to a conversation about meals • Read a report about food in the UK • Listen to a description of someone's day • *Story: The Silent Powers* Chapter 4 • *Life and culture*: My name is Dion	• Describe your habits • Talk about things you eat and drink • Write a report about food • Ask for and tell the time • Describe daily routines
Review	*Study skills:* How do you learn? *How's it going?:* Progress check *Coursework:* A day in my life			

	Grammar	Vocabulary and Pronunciation	Listening and Reading skills	Communicative tasks
Module 4 Inside and outside — **Unit 7 At home**	• *There is/are* • Uncountable nouns • Prepositions	• Homes • Things in a room • Food • *Rhythm drill:* stress in sentences	• Read a shopping list • Listen to a conversation in a supermarket • *Story: The Silent Powers* Chapter 5 • *Life and culture:* Homes in the UK	• Describe different homes • Write a description of your dream home • Ask about places and food • Write a 'disgusting recipe' • Describe a room
Unit 8 Having fun	• *Can* for ability and possibility • *I can see, I can hear* • *Must, mustn't* • Imperative	• Abilities • Places in a town • *Can* [æ], *can't* [ɑː], weak form of *can* [ə]	• Listen to and understand a song • Read a newspaper article • Read a poem • *Story: The Silent Powers* Chapter 6 • *Life and culture:* Stephen Hawking	• Talk about your abilities • Make a notice for a club • Describe things you can do in your town • Describe the sights and sounds around you • Tell people what to do • Write a short poem
Review	*Study skills:* Learning vocabulary	*How's it going?:* Progress check	*Coursework:* My neighbourhood	
Module 5 Today and tomorrow — **Unit 9 At the moment**	• Present continuous: affirmative, negative, questions, short answers • Object pronouns	• Clothes • Football • *Rhythm drill: -ing* [ɪŋ]	• Listen to a football commentary • Read about the World Cup • Listen to a conversation at a football stadium • *Story: The Silent Powers* Chapter 7 • *Life and culture:* Sports fans	• Describe things in progress at the moment • Play a guessing game • Describe what you're wearing now, and what you usually wear
Unit 10 Plans	• Present continuous used for the future • Suggestions • The future with *going to*	• Future time expressions • The weather • Weak form of *to* [tə] in *going to*	• Read a list of items in a café and a shop • Listen to and understand a song • Read a postcard • *Story: The Silent Powers* Chapter 8 • *Life and culture:* An exchange visit	• Talk about future arrangements • Make and reply to suggestions • Write a message to a friend • Describe plans and intentions • Talk about the weather • Write a holiday postcard
Review	*Study skills:* Parts of speech	*How's it going?:* Progress check	*Coursework:* My clothes	
Module 6 Looking back — **Unit 11 About the past**	• Past simple of *be* and regular verbs: affirmative, *Wh-* questions	• Occupations • *Rhythm drill:* verbs + *-ed* [t] [d] [ɪd]	• Listen to a conversation with a ghost • Read dictionary definitions • *Story: The Silent Powers* Chapter 9 • *Life and culture:* From North to South	• Talk about people from the past • Play a quiz game • Write about an imaginary person's life • Describe your early childhood
Unit 12 Heroes	• Past simple: negatives, questions, short answers; irregular verbs	• Past time expressions • Words with the same vowel sound	• Listen to a list of events in the past • Read an advertisement • Listen to and understand a song • *Story: The Silent Powers* Chapter 10 • *Life and culture:* Quiz: The UK and the USA	• Describe things that happened in the past • Write a letter about an event in the past • Write a diary • Talk about your school year
Review	*Study skills:* Planning your learning	*How's it going?:* Progress check	*Coursework:* My life line	

• Grammar index • Communicative functions index • Wordlist • Spelling notes • Lexical sets and irregular verbs • Songs

Module 1

Facts

In Module 1 you study

Grammar

- Sentences that you know in English
- Punctuation
- Personal questions and answers
- The verb *be*
- *Wh-* questions
- Singular and plural nouns

Vocabulary

- Words that you know in English
- Classroom language
- Numbers and dates
- The alphabet
- Names of members of a band
- Names of interests and activities
- Names of places around the world
- Geography vocabulary

so that you can

- Make sentences in English
- Tell the class about yourself
- Talk to your teacher in English
- Understand a letter in English
- Ask and answer questions about you
- Understand and use numbers
- Say the date
- Spell words in English
- Ask for permission and help
- Ask for and give information
- Write about an imaginary pop group
- Ask and answer questions about your interests
- Talk about facts
- Play a quiz game

Alphabet world

How many letters are there in your alphabet?

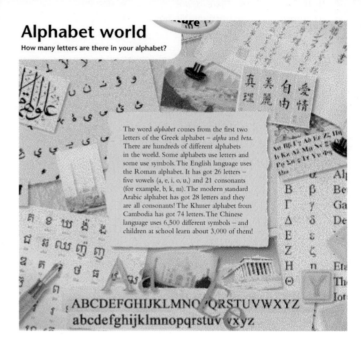

The word *alphabet* comes from the first two letters of the Greek alphabet – *alpha* and *beta*. There are hundreds of different alphabets in the world. Some alphabets use letters and some use symbols. The English language uses the Roman alphabet. It has got 26 letters – five vowels (a, e, i, o, u,) and 21 consonants (for example, b, k, m). The modern standard Arabic alphabet has got 28 letters and they are all consonants! The Khmer alphabet from Cambodia has got 74 letters. The Chinese language uses 6,500 different symbols – and children at school learn about 3,000 of them!

Life and culture

Alphabet world
The UK

Coursework 1

Facts about me
You write about your name, your interests and your school.

My name is Jack Ellis. I'm thirteen years old. My birthday is on 2nd October. I live with my mum in Exeter. I like computer games and books about animals.

My address is 20 Maple Road, Exeter, Devon EX11 4NP. My telephone number is: 0

What's it about?

What can you say about the pictures?

Now match the pictures with sentences 1–4.

1   A message in a bottle.
2   Meet Joe, Sadie, Sam and Jack!
3   Are they good at surfing?
4   What's the capital of Canada?

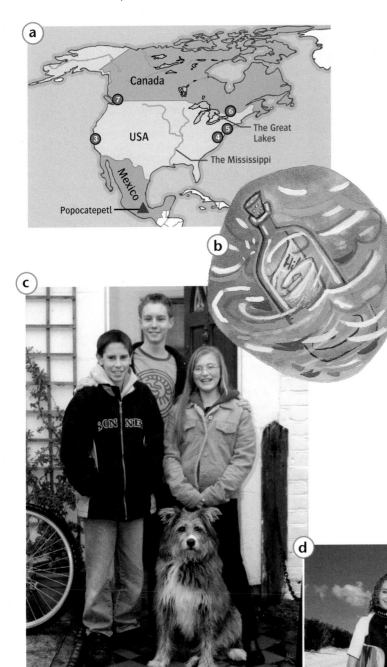

Coursework
All about me

In Book 1 you study
- the language of everyday life

so that you can
- describe yourself and your everyday life and complete an English Coursework folder.

Your Coursework has got six parts:

Part 1 Facts about me
You write about your name and age, where you live, your interests and your school.

Part 2 Important things to me
You write about your favourite people, places and things.

Part 3 A day in my life
You write about a typical day.

Part 4 My neighbourhood
You draw a map of your neighbourhood and describe places near your house.

Part 5 My clothes
You describe the sort of clothes you like, and the things you usually wear.

Part 6 My life line
You write about important events in your life.

1 What do you remember?

In Step 1 you study
- words and sentences that you know in English
- punctuation

so that you can
- make sentences in English
- tell the class about yourself

1 Words

a ⏱ Write the alphabet (A, B, C ...) in your notebook. Try to find an English word for each letter. You've got five minutes!

Apple   Bag   Cat   Desk
E...   F...

b Use words from your list and make groups of words on the board.

Animals	Food
elephant	pizza
cat	apple
	banana

Days	Things in a classroom
Monday	bag
Tuesday	desk

2 Sentences

a Look at the words in the balloons. How many sentences can you make?

I've got a bike.

b **What about you?** Make true sentences about you. Tell the class.

Hi! My name's Roberto. I like sport and computers.

Hello! I'm Maria. I'm twelve.

3 Listening *Song*

a Before you listen, look at the letters in the sea and make three words from the song. What do you think the song is about?

b 🔊 Listen to the song. Then put the words in the right order and make sentences from the song.

1 *What is it?*

1 it / what / is ?
2 sea / a / in / it's / the / bottle / in / message / a
3 in / it's / English
4 you / do / understand ?

🔊 Listen again and check.

4 Punctuation

a Complete the sentences in the box.

> **.** full stop **,** comma **?** question mark
> **!** exclamation mark **B** capital letter
>
> *We use a _____ at the beginning of a sentence.*
> *We use a _____ , a _____ or an _____ at the end.*
> *We use a _____ in the middle of a sentence.*

b Check the punctuation in your sentences in 3b.

5 Writing *Information about me*

Use what you know

Write at least five sentences about you. Make sure your punctuation is correct.

My name's Laura. I've got a cat.

In Step 2 you study
- classroom language
- personal information

so that you can
- talk to your teacher in English
- understand a letter in English
- ask and answer personal questions

1 Classroom language

a What can you do when you don't understand?

> Ask the teacher.

b What can you say when you don't understand?

> I don't understand.

c Think of more examples, then check the box.

When you don't understand ...

- Ask the teacher.
- Ask a friend.
- Use a dictionary.
- Try to guess.
- Don't panic!
- Say:
  I don't understand.
  Pardon? Can you say that again!
  What does ... mean?
  Can you help me?

2 Reading
A message in a bottle

a Read the message. Find words that you don't understand and use the ideas in 1c.

> What does 'best wishes' mean?

> I don't know. Ask the teacher.

b Can you guess these words?

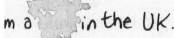

m a ▨ in the UK.

18 Maple Road
Exeter EX11 4NP
UK
30th August

Hi!
This is a letter from a ▨ in the UK. I'm English. I live in Exeter, in the southwest of ▨land. I'm tw▨. I like mu▨ and I'm interested in c▨ters.

I've got a brother and a s▨er. We've got ▨ dog called Sam and a tortoise c▨ Lightning.

What about you? What n▨lity are you? Where do you live? How old are you? W▨t's your ▨me?

Please write to me.
With best wishes from

3 Meet Joe, Sadie, Sam and Jack!

a 🔊 Close your book and listen to Joe, Sadie and Jack. Who is the message in the bottle from?

Hello! I'm Joe. I live in Exeter, at number eighteen Maple Road. I like music and I'm in a band. This is my sister. Her name's Sadie.

Hi! My name's Jack. I live next door to Sadie, at number twenty. I'm interested in computers and I like animals.

Hi! I'm Sadie, and this is our dog Sam. I'm twelve. My brother's fourteen and my sister Kate's eighteen. She's at university.

b 🔊 Listen again and follow in your book. Then complete the information.

The message is from .... because he/she is .... years old.
He/She has got ....
His/Her address is ....

c 🔊 Close your book and listen to the message in the bottle.

Remember!

Her name's Sadie. **She's** twelve.
His name's Joe. **He's** fourteen.

4 Writing and speaking *More about me*

Use what you know

Look at the questions at the end of the letter in 2b and write your answers. Then work with a friend and ask and answer.

What nationality are you?

I'm Argentinian.

STEP 3

In Step 3 you study
- numbers and dates
- the alphabet
- classroom language

so that you can
- understand and use numbers
- say the date

- spell words in English
- ask for permission and help

1 Numbers

a Say the numbers, then say the next number in the series.

```
1   1   3   5   7   ...9...
2   2   4   6   8   ...........
3   11  12  13      ...........
4   20  30          ...........
5   65  70  75      ...........
6   21  28  35      ...........
```

 Listen and check.

b Test a friend
Write another series of numbers. Read the numbers to a friend. Can your friend say the next number?

4, 8, 12 ...

2 Dates

Answer the questions.

SEPTEMBER

25

It's the twenty-fifth of September.

1 What's the date today?
2 When's your national day?

Remember!

We write: 25th September
We say: the twenty-fifth **of** September

See page 143 for dates and months.

3 The alphabet

a Say the letters in each group.

Kate /eɪ/
A H K

Lee /iː/
B C E
P T V

Mel /e/
F L M
X Z

Mike /aɪ/
I

Joe /əʊ/
O

Sue /uː/
Q W

Mark /ɑː/
R

b Now put these letters in the right group. *D – Lee*
D G J N S U Y
 Listen and check.

4 Things in the classroom

a Say the names of at least two things in the classroom.

Window, dictionary.

b Listen and write the letters. *1 R–U–L–E–R*
Now say the words.

Ruler ...

Revision

5 Asking for permission

a Match the questions with the pictures.

1 Can I use your ruler, please?
2 Can I look at your dictionary, please?
3 Can I close the window, please?

b Ask and answer the questions in 5a.

> Can I look at your dictionary, please?

> Yes, of course. / No, sorry.

c If you have time, make more questions:

Can I use your rubber, please?

6 Asking for help

a What can you say about the photos?

b 🔊 Close your book and listen. What homework has Jack got?

SADIE: Hello. 802465.
JACK: Hi, Sadie. It's Jack. How are you?
SADIE: All right, thanks.
JACK: Sadie, can you help me with my homework?
SADIE: Sure.
JACK: How do you say 'It's great' in French?
SADIE: *C'est chouette.*
JACK: How do you spell it?
SADIE: I think it's C - apostrophe - E - S - T, C - H - O - U - E - double T - E.
JACK: Thanks, Sadie.
SADIE: That's OK. See you tomorrow, Jack. Bye!

c 🔊 Listen again and follow in your book. Then put the words in the right order. Ask and answer the questions.

1 say / language / do / how / in / you / 'It's great' / your ?
2 you / 'great' / how / do / spell ?

d **Role play** If you have time, act the conversation between Jack and Sadie. Change some details if you like.

7 Writing *A letter to Sadie*

Use what you know

Look at the letter on page 8, then write a reply.
Use words from Steps 1 and 2.

> (Your address)
> (The date)
>
> Dear Sadie,
> I've got your message! My name's .... I live in .... I ....
> With best wishes from ....

If you aren't sure, ask your teacher.

> How do you spell 'hamster' ? How do you say ... in English?

Revision

Extra exercises

1 Put the words in the right order and make questions.

1 What's your name?

1 your / what / name / 's ?
2 do / name / spell / you / how / your ?
3 mean / it / what / does ?
4 me / can / help / you ?
5 it / what / is ?
6 you / are / how ?
7 use / can / rubber / I / your ?
8 understand / do / you ?

2 Complete the conversations.

1 a

1 How are you?
  a All right, thanks.
  b I'm James.
  c He's fine.

2 Can you help me?
  a That's OK.
  b Sure.
  c Fine, thanks.

3 Can I look at your dictionary?
  a Yes, please.
  b All right, thanks.
  c Yes, of course.

4 Thanks, Jack.
  a That's OK.
  b It's great.
  c No, sorry.

5 Can I look at your answers?
  a No, thanks.
  b No, sorry.
  c I'm all right.

3 Choose the right word. *1 b*

1 My _____ is Sadie.
  a surname   b name   c nationality

2 This is Joe. He's _____ .
  a England   b English   c the UK

3 Hello, I'm Jack. I'm _____ .
  a friend   b thirteen   c sister

4 Can you _____ me with my homework?
  a read   b help   c write

5 I'm interested in music and _____ .
  a computer   b a computer   c computers

4 Write the answers.

1 $50 - 10 =$ *forty*
2 $10 + 12 + 15 =$ _____
3 $10 \times 5 =$ _____
4 $40 - 17 =$ _____
5 $10 + 7 =$ _____
6 $2 \times 7 =$ _____
7 $14 + 5 =$ _____
8 $90 - 10 + 10 =$ _____
9 $75 - 11 =$ _____
10 $22 \times 4 =$ _____

5 Which word is the odd one out? *1 brother*

1 brother   elephant   tortoise   dog
2 pizza   apple   teacher   banana
3 Monday   Thursday   September   Wednesday
4 desk   computer   sea   ruler
5 comma   university   full stop   question mark

6 How do you say these sentences in your language?

1 How do you spell 'Kate'?
2 What does 'guess' mean?
3 I don't understand.
4 Can you say that again?
5 Can you help me?
6 Can I use your dictionary?

Life and culture

Alphabet world

How many letters are there in your alphabet?

The word *alphabet* comes from the first two letters of the Greek alphabet – *alpha* and *beta*. There are hundreds of different alphabets in the world. Some alphabets use letters and some use symbols. The English language uses the Roman alphabet. It has got 26 letters – five vowels (a, e, i, o, u,) and 21 consonants (for example, b, k, m). The modern standard Arabic alphabet has got 28 letters and they are all consonants! The Khmer alphabet from Cambodia has got 74 letters. The Chinese language uses 6,500 different symbols – and children at school learn about 3,000 of them!

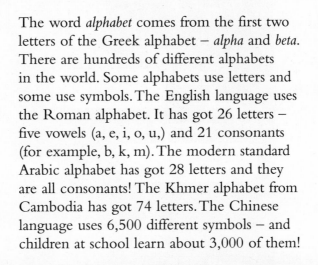

ABCDEFGHIJKLMNOPQRSTUVWXYZ
abcdefghijklmnopqrstuvwxyz

ABOUT ALPHABETS

Runes are an old and mysterious alphabet from Northern Europe.

Tolkien uses the runic alphabet in his books *The Lord of the Rings* and *The Hobbit*.

Task

Are these sentences true or false?

1 False.

1 All alphabets in the world use letters.
2 There are 26 letters in the English language.
3 The Arabic alphabet has got 28 consonants.
4 The Khmer alphabet is from Europe.
5 The Chinese language has got 3,000 symbols.

In Step 1 you study
- names of members of a band
- the verb *be*: affirmative
- *Wh-* questions

so that you can
- ask for and give information
- write about an imaginary pop group

1 Key vocabulary
Members of a band

a Match the words with the numbers in the photo.

1 keyboard player

singer   drummer
bass guitarist
lead guitarist
keyboard player

b 🔊 Listen to Joe and his band. Then use the words in 1a and complete the sentences 1–5.

Hi! Do you remember me? I'm Joe Kelly. This is my band, Monsoon. Come and meet the others. Come and listen!

3 I'm Lee. I'm the ....

2 I'm Sadie. I'm the ....

1 I'm the keyboard player .

4 My name's Mel. I'm the ....

5 And my name's Barney. I'm the ....

A new school band!

by Mel Adams

There is an exciting new band at the school! It's called Monsoon. Joe Kelly is the leader, and he's the keyboard player. Sadie Kelly is the drummer. She's only 12 but she's brilliant! I'm the singer. The other two members of the group are Lee Harper and Barney Sutton. They're the two guitarists. Lee is the bass guitarist, and Barney is the lead guitarist. We're all students at Westover School. We need another singer! If you're interested, contact me! I'm in Class 9Y.

2 Presentation   *It's called Monsoon*

a Read the text. What is it?

a   a letter from Mel Adams
b   an article in a school magazine
c   an article by a teacher at Westover School

b 🔊 Listen and follow the text in your book. Then match the questions with the answers.   1 c

1   Who's the singer?
2   Who's the drummer?
3   Who are the two guitarists?
4   Where are they from?
5   What's the name of the band?

a   Westover School.
b   Monsoon.
c   Mel Adams.
d   Lee Harper and Barney Sutton.
e   Sadie Kelly.

Ask and answer the questions.

3 Key grammar be: *affirmative*

Copy and complete the table. Use short forms from the article in Exercise 2.

Full form	Short form	
Singular		
I am	I'm	
You are	....	
He is	....	brilliant!
She is	....	
It is	....	
Plural		
We are	....	
You are	....	brilliant!
They are	....	

G ➔ 2a

4 Practice

Complete the sentences.

1 This is Joe. __He's__ the leader of Monsoon.
2 My name's Sadie. .... a student.
3 I like Alicia Keys. .... my favourite singer.
4 Lee and Joe are friends. .... in Class 9SJ.
5 Jack and I are students. .... at Westover School.
6 Barney, look at the time! .... late!
7 Mel and Lee, ... late!
8 This is my keyboard. .... Japanese.

5 Key grammar

Wh- *questions*

How do you say *What, Where, Who* and *When* in your language?

> **What's** the name of the band?
> **Where's** Exeter?
> **Who's** the drummer?
> **When's** your national day?

G ➔ 14

6 Practice

a Complete the questions with *What, Where, Who* or *When*.

1 __What__'s your name?
2 ....'s your birthday?
3 .... are you from?
4 ....'s your English teacher?
5 ....'s your address?

b **What about you?** Work with a friend and ask and answer the questions in 6a.

(What's your name?)   (My name's Maria.)

7 Reading and speaking
Band practice

Try this!
We normally say:
I am ... and *He is ...* .
Can we say: *I is ... ?*

a Read the email. Who is it from?

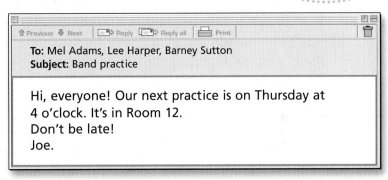

To: Mel Adams, Lee Harper, Barney Sutton
Subject: Band practice

Hi, everyone! Our next practice is on Thursday at 4 o'clock. It's in Room 12.
Don't be late!
Joe.

b Complete the conversation. Then ask and answer the questions.

A: When's the next practice?
B: It's on .... at ....
A: Where is it?
B: It's in ....

c If you have time, make another conversation.

(When's our next football practice?)

(It's on Friday at five o'clock.)

8 Speaking and writing *My new band*

Use what you know

Imagine you're in a band with your friends, or with your favourite stars. Copy and complete the list, then ask your classmates about their bands.

The band is called ...   Singer: ...
Lead guitarist: ...   Bass guitarist: Me
Drummer: ...   Keyboard player: ...

Now write a description of your band. Use words from the article by Mel in Exercise 2.

G ➔ *When you see this, look at the Grammar notes at the back of the Workbook.*

In Step 2 you study
- the verb *be*: negative; questions and short answers
- names of interests and activities

so that you can
- ask and answer questions about your interests

1 Presentation *Are they good at sport?*

a What can you say about the photos?

Dear Sadie,

Hi! How are you? It's re
here in Sydney so Mar
go to the beach every
school. I hope you like
photo! I've got a new
it's great.

b 🔊 Close your book and listen to the conversation between Sadie and Jack. What's the capital of Australia?

It's 8.15 in the morning. Sadie and Jack are at the bus stop.

SADIE: I've got a letter from my cousin, and a photo. Look! That's Annie.
JACK: She's nice.
SADIE: And that's Mark.
JACK: Is he her boyfriend?
SADIE: No, he isn't. He's her brother.
JACK: What a fantastic beach! Is it in England?
SADIE: No, it's in Australia. They live in Sydney.
JACK: Are they good at surfing?
SADIE: Yes, they are. And they're good at volleyball and tennis and swimming!
JACK: Is Sydney the capital of Australia?
SADIE: No, it isn't. Canberra's the capital.
JACK: Oh yes. I'm not very good at geography, and I'm not very good at sport.
SADIE: Never mind, Jack. No one's perfect.

c 🔊 Listen again and follow in your book. Then choose the right answer to the questions. *1 b*

1 Is Sadie with her cousin?
  a Yes, it is.
  b No, she isn't.
  c Yes, she is.
2 Are Jack and Sadie on the beach?
  a No, they aren't.
  b Yes, we are.
  c Yes, they are.
3 Is Canberra the capital of Australia?
  a Yes, she is.
  b Yes, he is.
  c Yes, it is.

2 Key grammar be: *negative; questions and short answers*

Complete the answers.

> **I'm not** good at sport.
> **He isn't** her boyfriend.
> **They aren't** English.
>
> **Are you** good at sport?
> _____ , **I am.** / _____ , **I'm not.**
>
> **Is he** her brother?
> Yes, **he is.** / No, **he** _____ .
>
> **Are they** Australian?
> Yes, **they** _____ . / No, **they aren't.**

G ➔ 2b, c, e

3 Practice

a Complete the questions.

1 __*Are*__ you good at English?
2 _____ Jack good at sport?
3 _____ Sydney in Australia?
4 _____ it the capital?
5 _____ Jack and Sadie in Sydney?

b Ask and answer the questions in 3a.

(Are you good at English?) (Yes, I am.)

c **Test a friend** Write at least one question with *Is/Are ...?* Can your friend answer the question?

(Are Joe and Sadie Australian?)

(No, they aren't.)

4 Key vocabulary *Interests and activities*

Match the words with the pictures. *1 computer games*

sport   art   computer games   science   cooking   reading   music   swimming

🔊 Listen and check.

5 Reading and listening *A survey*

a Read the Student Survey. What is the survey about?

WESTOVER SCHOOL MAGAZINE Student Survey
What are you good at? What are you interested in? We want to know!

Name *Jack Ellis*   Class   *8NT*

Are you good at	Yes, I am.	I'm not bad.	No, I'm not.
• sport?	☐	☐	✓
• art?	☐	✓	☐
• computer games?	✓	☐	☐
• swimming?	☐	☐	✓

Are you interested in	Yes, I am.	I'm quite interested.	No, I'm not.
• science?	✓	☐	☐
• cooking?	☐	✓	☐
• reading?	☐	✓	☐
• music?	✓	☐	☐

b 🔊 Listen to Mel and Jack. Look at Jack's answers. Which tick (✓) is in the wrong place?

c Make at least three true sentences about Jack.

He isn't bad at art.
He's quite interested in cooking.

6 Writing and speaking

a **What about you?** Look at the survey. Write at least three true sentences about you.

I'm not bad at sport.
I'm quite interested in science.

b Work with a friend. Ask and answer questions from the survey.

A: Are you good at computer games?
B: I'm not bad.
A: Are you interested in music?
B: Yes, I am.

7 Speaking *My interests*

Use what you know

Work with a friend. Ask and answer questions about other interests.

Are you good at football?
Are you interested in animals?

Tell the class about your friend.

Paul's good at football.
He's interested in cars, but he isn't interested in animals.

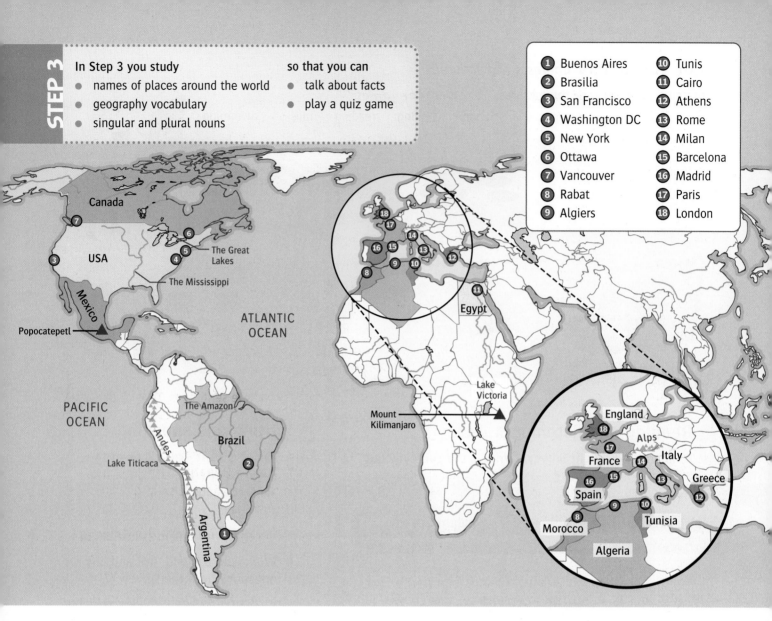

In Step 3 you study
- names of places around the world
- geography vocabulary
- singular and plural nouns

so that you can
- talk about facts
- play a quiz game

1. Buenos Aires
2. Brasilia
3. San Francisco
4. Washington DC
5. New York
6. Ottawa
7. Vancouver
8. Rabat
9. Algiers
10. Tunis
11. Cairo
12. Athens
13. Rome
14. Milan
15. Barcelona
16. Madrid
17. Paris
18. London

1 Key vocabulary *Countries and cities*

Cover the map. What countries and capital cities do you know in English?

England, Argentina, Madrid, London

2 Key pronunciation

Word stress

a 🔊 Listen to the rhythm drill, then join in.

Listen to the words.
Listen to the beat.
Clap your hands and stamp your feet.
Rome! Spain! France! Greece!
London! **Eng**land! **Pa**ris! **Eu**rope!
Washington! **It**aly! **Ca**nada! **Am**azon!
Titi**ca**ca! Missi**ssi**ppi! Argen**ti**na! Barce**lo**na!
Kiliman**ja**ro! Kiliman**ja**ro!
Popoca**pe**tl! Popoca**pe**tl!

b 🔊 Listen to the names and match them with their stress patterns. *England – 2*

England	1	●
America	2	●●●
Kilimanjaro	3	●●●●
Spain	4	●●●●●
Africa	5	●●●●●●

3 Writing and speaking

a 🕐 Look at the map. How many facts can you find? You've got three minutes!

Washington is the capital of the USA.
The Andes are in South America.

b Ask and answer questions about the map.

What's the capital of Italy?

Where are the Great Lakes?

4 Key vocabulary *Geography*

Look at the words and the photos.
Ask and answer.

> What's number one?

> It's a mountain.

Singular	Plural
lake	lakes
mountain	mountains
volcano	volcanoes
river	rivers
hill	hills
city	cities
country	countries

See *Spelling notes, page 142.*

 Listen and check.

5 Listening *A radio quiz*

> I'm interested in geography and my favourite radio programme is *Is that right?* Listen!

a 📼 Copy the words in Exercise 4. Then listen to the radio quiz and tick (✓) the words you hear.

b 📼 Read the sentences. Then listen to the quiz again. Are the sentences right or wrong?

1 Madrid is the capital of Italy.
2 Kilimanjaro isn't a city.
3 Vancouver and Brasilia are countries.
4 The Thames and the Mississippi aren't lakes.
5 The Great Lakes aren't in Europe.

c How do you say these expressions in your language?

1 Are you ready?
2 Is it right or wrong?
3 Are you sure?
4 Well done!
5 I'm sorry.
6 Yes, please.
7 Oh dear!

6 Speaking *A quiz*

Use what you know

Play *Is that right?* Use the expressions in 5c.

Use names on the map, or talk about places in your country.

A: Milan and Madrid are capital cities.
B: Wrong!
A: The Andes aren't in Spain.
B: Right!

Find some new ideas.

A: Hondas are Italian.
B: Wrong!
A: Beckham is a footballer.
B: Right!

Extra exercises

1 Complete the conversations.
1 a

1 Are you good at sport?
  a I'm not bad.
  b I'm quite interested.
  c Yes, he is.

2 Are you interested in cooking?
  a Yes, I am.
  b No, she isn't.
  c That's OK.

3 Where's the next practice?
  a At four o'clock.
  b In Room 12.
  c On Wednesday.

4 Who's her boyfriend?
  a In Australia.
  b Her name's Kim.
  c Barney Sutton.

2 Choose the right word. 1 c

1 Rome and Paris are ....
  a countries
  b volcanoes
  c cities

2 Britain is a ....
  a nationality
  b country
  c language

3 Volleyball is my favourite ....
  a animal
  b music
  c sport

4 Mel is a singer in a ....
  a band
  b class
  c magazine

5 The Mississippi is a ....
  a lake
  b river
  c hill

3 Complete the conversation from the radio programme *Is that right?*
1 c

A: Are you ready to play *Is that right?*
B: [1] ....
A: Listen carefully. Is it right or wrong? Vancouver is a country.
B: [2] ....
A: Yes. And you've got £1,000.
B: [3] ....
A: Now listen carefully. Canberra is in Australia.
B: [4] ....
A: Oh John, I'm sorry. Yes, it is. It's the capital.
B: [5] ....

a Great!

b Oh well, never mind. I've got £1,000.

c Yes, Danny.

d Wrong. It's a city.

e Er ... I'm not sure. No, it isn't.

4 Complete the words.

1 Sadie is the d _rummer_ in the band Monsoon.
2 Perth isn't the c............ of Australia.
3 Vesuvius is a famous v............ in Italy.
4 Monsoon is the name of a b............ .
5 Beckham is good at f............ .
6 Joe is the l............ of Monsoon.
7 He's a s............ at Westover School.

5 Make questions for these answers. Use *Who, Where, What* or *When*.
1 *When is Christmas Day?*

1 It's on 25th December.
2 It's in Australia.
3 53, Albany Road, Bristol.
4 He's the lead guitarist of Monsoon.
5 It's on 12th April.

6 How do you say these sentences in your language?

1 Never mind.
2 Well done!
3 Oh dear!
4 Are you ready?
5 Is he good at surfing?
6 What a fantastic beach!

Extra reading

The UK

How many countries are there in the United Kingdom? Read the text and find out.

ABOUT THE UK

Britain's favourite food is *Chicken Tikka Masala* – an Indian curry.

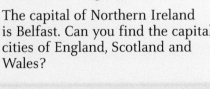

Edinburgh

Lough Erne Belfast

Manchester

Birmingham   Leicester

Cardiff   London

Channel Tunnel

CORNWALL

W hat is the difference between England, Great Britain and the United Kingdom? You don't know? Well, don't worry, because a lot of British people aren't sure of the answer. It's complicated!

England, Scotland and Wales are three separate countries, but they have all got the same prime minister and nearly everyone speaks English. The three countries together are called Great Britain.

To the west of Great Britain is Ireland. Northern Ireland and the three countries of Great Britain are called the United Kingdom.

The capital of Northern Ireland is Belfast. Can you find the capital cities of England, Scotland and Wales?

Task

Match the sentences with the pictures on the map.

1   You can hear Caribbean music at a famous carnival here.
2   A beautiful lake and a great place for fishing!
3   Are you interested in football? This is the place for you!
4   Hello, my name's Rajid. We've got a restaurant here.
5   There's a famous festival of music and theatre here every August.
6   The Tanveer family are Muslim. They go to the mosque every Friday.
7   It connects the UK to France.
8   A popular area for water sports.

Unit 2   21

Module 1 Review

Language summary

1 The English alphabet

A B C D E F G H I J K L M N
O P Q R S T U V W X Y Z

Check that you can

1.1 ● say the colours and match the sound with the groups of letters. *red – LNS*

green red grey blue yellow white
LNS IY QU BDV O AHK

1.2 ● ask and say how to spell English words.

> How do you spell 'dictionary'?

> D - I - C - T - I - O - N - A - R - Y

2 Numbers

Check that you can

2.1 ● ask about age and say your age.

> How old are you? I'm twelve.

2.2 ● count backwards from 30 to 10.

> Thirty, twenty-nine, ...

See Numbers, page 143.

3 Dates

Check that you can

3.1 ● say today's date.

> It's the twelfth of October.

3.2 ● say the date of your birthday.

> When's your birthday?

> It's on the twenty-first of April.

See Months and Days, page 143.

4 Can I ... , please?

Check that you can

● ask for permission.

Put the words in the right order and make three questions.

1 ruler / use / I / your / can ?
2 I / close / can / please / window / the ?
3 look at / can / dictionary / your / I / please ?

5 The verb *be*

Affirmative			Negative	
I'm			I'm not	
You're	Italian.		You aren't	English.
He's			He isn't	
She's	Spanish.		She isn't	at home.
It's			It isn't	
We're	at school.		We aren't	sure.
You're			You aren't	
They're	thirteen.		They aren't	

I'm = I am   You're = You are   He's = He is
aren't = are not   isn't = is not

Questions

Am I		Yes, you are.
	late?	No, you aren't.
Are you		Yes, I am.
		No, I'm not.
Is he/she/it		Yes, he/she/it is.
	right?	No, he/she/it isn't.
Are we		Yes, you are.
		No, you aren't.
Are you	ready?	Yes, we are.
		No, we aren't.
Are they		Yes, they are.
		No, they aren't.

You is singular and plural:
*Jack, are **you** ready?*
*Jack and Sadie, are **you** ready?*
The form: *you are / you're* is the same.

What		an anaconda?
Where	is	Timbuktu?
When		Christmas Day?
Who	are	the Corrs?

Check that you can

5.1 ● talk about facts. Make true sentences.

I'm 12. Barcelona is in Spain.
The Andes are in South America.

5.2 ● ask and answer questions like these.

Are you interested in music?
Is Sydney in Australia?

5.3 ● understand and ask questions with *What*, *Where*, *When* and *Who*.

Make four questions from the table on page 22, then match them with these answers.

1 It's on the twenty-fifth of December.
2 It's a snake.
3 They're pop stars.
4 It's in Africa.

Now complete these questions. Do you know the answers?

1 .... Pavarotti?
2 .... the Alps?
3 .... a BMW?
4 .... New Year's Day?
5 .... the Simpsons?
6 .... Paris?

6 Plural nouns

Lee is a guitarist.
Lee and Barney are guitarist**s**.

The Thames is a river.
The Thames and the Mississippi are river**s**.

Check that you can

● say these words in the plural.

mountain   lake   city   country   student
volcano

See Spelling notes, page 142.

7 Prepositions *in, on, at*

I live **in** Exeter.
Exeter is **in** England.
Our band practice is **in** Room 12.
The song is **in** English.

My birthday is **on** 3rd January.
See you **on** Sunday.

Please come **at** eight o'clock.
Mel is **at** Westover School.
We live **at** number 18.

Check that you can use the correct preposition for

7.1 ● dates:

Christmas is .... the twenty-fifth of December.

7.2 ● days:

The concert is .... Saturday.

7.3 ● times:

Our English lesson is .... ten o'clock.

7.4 ● places:

1 They live .... Ottawa. It's .... Canada.
2 My bag is .... the classroom.
3 Sadie and Jack are .... Westover School.

8 Capital letters

We use a capital letter to begin the names of:

> **Cities and countries:** Tokyo, Spain
> **Nationalities and languages:** English, Italian
> **Days of the week:** Monday, Saturday
> **Months:** January, April

Check that you can

● say which words begin with a capital letter.

yellow   japanese   monday   june   french
teacher   washington   lake   month   august
italy   thursday   spanish   argentina   day

9 Classroom language

Check that you can

● understand these sentences.

> Look at the photos.
> Listen to the CD/cassette.
> Read the conversation.
> Write true sentences.
> Ask your teacher.
> Ask/Answer the questions.
> Work with a partner.
> Make a list.
> Say 'hippopotamus'.
>
> Is it right or wrong?
> Jack's right. Sadie's wrong.
> The right answer. / The wrong answer.
>
> I'm sure. / I'm not sure. I know. / I don't know.
> I understand. / I don't understand. I think ... .
>
> What does 'guess' mean?
> How do you say ... in English?
> How do you spell 'eight'?
> Pardon? Can you say that again?
> Can you help me, please?
> Can I use your dictionary?

Vocabulary

Personal information

I'm American.
I live in New York.
I've got two sisters.
I'm interested in surfing.
I'm quite good at sport.

Music

band
drummer
guitarist
bass guitarist
lead guitarist
keyboard player
leader
singer

Subjects and interests

art
computer games
cooking
football
geography
music
reading
science
sport
surfing
swimming
tennis
volleyball

Geography

beach
capital
city
country
hill
lake
mountain
river
sea
town
volcano

Expressions

Are you ready?
Are you sure?
Don't panic!
How are you?
Fine. / I'm fine. / All right, thanks.
Never mind.
Oh dear!
Pardon?
See you tomorrow / on Sunday.
Sorry. / I'm sorry.
Thanks. / Thank you.
Thanks very much.
That's OK.
Well done!
What a fantastic beach!
What about you?
Yes, of course.
Yes, please.

Study skills 1   Your coursebook

Can you answer these questions?

1   How many Units are there in the book?
2   How many Reviews are there?
3   Where is the Wordlist?
4   Where can you find information about grammar?
5   What page is Coursework 1 on?

How's it going?

Hi! How's it going? English isn't easy, so if you've got some problems, don't worry! No one's perfect! Ask a friend. Talk to someone who can speak English. And don't forget to tell your teacher!

● **Your rating**

Look again at pages 22–23. For each section give yourself a star rating:

Good ☆ ☆ ☆   Not bad ☆ ☆   I can't remember much ☆

● **Vocabulary**

Choose two titles in the Vocabulary list, then close your book. How many words can you remember for each topic?

● **Test a friend**

Look again at Units 1 and 2. Think of at least two questions about these units, then ask a friend.

How do you spell 'computer'?
Is Jack good at geography?

● **Write to your teacher**

Write a short letter to your teacher in your own language. Say how things are going. Have you got any problems?

● **Your Workbook**

Complete the Learning diaries for Units 1 and 2.

Coursework 1 – All about me!

Read about Jack. Then write about:

- your name, age and where you live
- your interests
- your address and telephone number
- your town
- your school.

Use drawings, pictures and photos too.

Facts about me

My name is Jack Ellis. I'm thirteen years old. My birthday is on 2nd October. I live with my mum in Exeter. I like computer games and books about animals.

My address is:
20 Maple Road,
Exeter,
Devon EX11 4NP.
My telephone number is: 01352 736459

River Exe

Exeter

Hi!

EXETER

Exeter is a town in the southwest of England. It's on the River Exe. It's quite near the sea.

I'm a student at Westover Comprehensive School. I'm in Class 8NT. I'm quite good at art and I'm interested in science. I'm not very good at sport.

This is a photo of me and my friend Ben with our skateboards at the skate park.

Module 2

Things and people

In Module 2 you study

Grammar

- *Have got + a/an; some/any*
- Possessive *'s*
- Possessive adjectives
- *This/these; that/those*
- *What is/are ... like?*
- *Has got*

Vocabulary

- Names of everyday things
- Names of the members of a family
- Adjectives
- Parts of the body
- Adjectives describing how you feel
- *I've got a headache/cold*

so that you can

- Talk about possessions, and things you use at school
- Identify things
- Say who something belongs to
- Write a description of a family
- Ask about and describe things
- Talk about a person's appearance and personality
- Say how you feel
- Write a description of an imaginary person

The Silent Powers

Chapter 1 – Two messages for Sophie
Chapter 2 – Sophie's dream

Life and culture

Collections
London

Coursework 2

Important things to me
You write about your favourite people, places and things.

26

What's it about?

What can you say about the pictures?

Now match the pictures with sentences 1–5.

1 I've got some cameras and some CDs.
2 Val is Robbie's grandmother.
3 My favourite TV programme is *Extreme Sports*.
4 He's got a cruel face and his teeth are black.
5 Is this your lunchbox?

What have you got?

In Step 1 you study
- names of everyday things
- *have got + a/an; some/any*

so that you can
- talk about possessions, and things you use at school

1 Key vocabulary *Everyday things*

Look at the things in the pictures.
How many words do you know?

1 key   2 CD player   3 watch

4 badges   5 tennis racket   6 crisps

7 anorak   8 tissues   9 umbrella

10 pencil case   11 calculator   12 peanuts

 Listen and say the words.

2 Presentation *Have you got any peanuts?*

a  Cover the text and listen to the conversation between Sadie and her friend Lisa. Where are they?

a in the park   b at school   c at the cinema

SADIE: Lisa! What's the time?
LISA: I don't know. I haven't got a watch. Sssh!
SADIE: Lisa! I'm hungry. Have you got any peanuts?
LISA: No, I haven't. But I've got some crisps in my bag. Here you are.
SADIE: Thanks. Mmm … These are nice.
MAN: Sssh!
SADIE: Sorry. Lisa!
LISA: What's the matter now?
SADIE: I haven't got any tissues.
LISA: What?
SADIE: Have you got any tissues?
LISA: Wait a minute. Yes, I have. Here you are.
WOMAN: Sssh!
LISA: Sorry.
SADIE: Lisa! Have you got my umbrella? I can't find it.
LISA: Never mind. Be quiet and watch the film.
MAN: Sssh! Can you be quiet, please!
LISA and SADIE: Sorry.

b Listen again and follow in your book. Then match the words in A with the words in B and make sentences.

1 *Have you got any peanuts?*

	A	B
1	Have you got any	watch.
2	I haven't got a	peanuts?
3	I haven't got	any tissues?
4	I've got	any tissues.
5	Have you got	some crisps.

c **Role play** If you have time, act the conversation between Sadie and Lisa.

3 Key grammar have got + a/an or some

Complete the explanation with *a*, *an* and *some*.

I've
You've
We've   got
They've

a watch / pencil case / CD player.
an umbrella/anorak/apple.
some peanuts/tissues/crisps.

*We use ..... or ..... with singular nouns
and ..... with plural nouns.*

Ⓖ➔ 10a, 15a–c

4 Practice

a Choose the right word.   *1 some*

1 You've got (*a / an / some*) computer games.
2 I've got (*a / an / some*) tennis racket.
3 They've got (*a / an / some*) badges.
4 We've got (*a / an / some*) umbrella.
5 You've got (*a / an / some*) CD player.

b Test a friend Write three sentences with *I've got*. Leave a blank for *a*, *an* or *some*. Can your friend complete the sentences?

I've got .... apple.

5 Speaking

What about you? Talk about your things.

I've got a key and some tissues in my pocket.

What have you got:
1 in your pocket?   2 on your desk?   3 in your bag?

6 Key pronunciation   *Plural nouns* /s/ /z/ /ɪz/

a 🔊 Listen to the rhythm drill, then join in.

I've got some badges and some watches,
some cameras and CDs,
some dictionaries and pencil cases,
mobiles and TVs.
I've got some skateboards and some trainers,
some socks and anoraks,
some T-shirts and umbrellas,
bags and baseball caps.

b 🔊 Listen and repeat the words.

1 /s/   T-shirts anoraks caps
2 /z/   bags cameras skateboards
3 /ɪz/ badges pencil cases watches

7 Key grammar   have got + some/any

Complete the explanation with *some* and *any*.

I've got **some** crisps.
I haven't got **any** crisps.

Have you got **any** crisps?
Yes, I have. / No, I haven't.

We use .... with plurals in affirmative sentences.
We use .... with plurals in negative sentences.
We normally use .... in questions.

Ⓖ➔ 10, 19

8 Practice

a What about you? Write true sentences with *I've got* or *I haven't got* and *some* or *any*.

1 I haven't got any badges.

1 badges   4 football socks
2 computer games 5 trainers
3 English books   6 CDs

b Ask your friends about the things in 8a.

Have you got any badges?

Yes, I have. / No, I haven't.

c If you have time, think of other things and make more questions.

Have you got a bike?   Yes, I have.

9 Writing and speaking   *My school shop*

Use what you know

Imagine there's a shop at your school. You're the manager! What have you got in your shop? Write at least two useful things and two interesting things.

I've got some dictionaries and ...

Work with a friend. Ask about his/her shop.

A: What have you got in your shop?
B: I've got some calculators, and I've got some baseball caps.
A: Have you got any computer games?
B: Yes, I have. / No, I haven't.

In Step 2 you study
- possessive 's
- possessive adjectives
- *this/these, that/those*

so that you can
- identify things
- say who something belongs to

1 Presentation
That's Joe's lunchbox

a What can you say about the photos?

b 🔊 Listen to the conversation and follow in your book. What are the names of the things (1–8) in the photos?

It's Monday morning. Sadie and Joe are with their father in the kitchen. Everyone is in a hurry.

MR KELLY: Is this your lunchbox, Sadie?

SADIE: No, I've got my lunchbox in my bag. That's Joe's lunchbox.

JOE: Where are my trainers, Dad?

MR KELLY: I don't know. Sue! Where are Joe's trainers?

MRS KELLY: His trainers and his football socks are on the stairs. And Sadie's umbrella and her watch are on the stairs too.

JOE: I'm hungry. Dad, are those your sandwiches?

MR KELLY: Yes, they are. Don't eat those! They're for my lunch.

SADIE: Telephone!

JOE: Oh, no! Where's my mobile?

SADIE: I don't know. I haven't got your mobile.

JOE: It's in my anorak. Where's my anorak?

SADIE: I can hear our bus. Come on, Joe, hurry up!

JOE: Hi, Barney … Sadie, wait a minute!

SADIE: Bye, Mum. Bye, Dad. Have a nice day.

c 🔊 Listen again. Are these sentences true or false? Correct the false sentences.

2 They're Joe's trainers.

1 It's Joe's lunchbox.
2 They're Sadie's trainers.
3 They're Mr Kelly's football socks.
4 It's Mrs Kelly's umbrella.
5 It's Sadie's watch.
6 They're Mr Kelly's sandwiches.
7 It's Sadie's mobile.
8 It's Joe's anorak.

2 Key grammar *Possessive 's*

How do you say these sentences in your language?

> Where are Joe**'s** trainers?
> Kate is Joe and Sadie**'s** sister.

 20

3 Practice

Match the words in A with the words in B and make sentences.

1 *Mike and Sue are Sadie's parents.*

	A	B
1	Mike and Sue	Sadie's tortoise
2	Joe	Sadie's parents
3	Sam	Lisa's best friend
4	Lightning	Kate's brother
5	Annie and Mark	Joe and Sadie's dog
6	Sadie	Joe and Sadie's cousins

4 Key grammar
Possessive adjectives

Complete the table with possessive adjectives from the conversation.

I	→	...my...
you	→	----------
he	→	----------
she	→	----------
we	→	----------
you	→	----------
they	→	*their*

G→ 21

5 Practice

Complete the sentences with possessive adjectives.

1 Sadie's lunchbox is in __her__ bag.
2 Joe hasn't got _____ trainers.
3 Sue is Joe and Sadie's mother and Mike is _____ father.
4 Joe's mobile is in _____ anorak.
5 Sadie's sandwiches are in _____ lunchbox.
6 Joe, have you got _____ anorak?

6 Listening
Two famous sisters

a What do you know about the women in the photo?

b 🔊 Listen to the information. Then match the questions with the answers. *1 c*

1 What are their names?
2 What's their surname?
3 Is that Venus on the right?
4 What's their father's name?
5 What's their mother's name?
6 What's their favourite place?

a His name's Richard.
b Their house in Florida.
c Venus and Serena.
d Her name's Oracene.
e No, that's her sister, Serena.
f Williams.

> **Remember!**
>
>
>
> A: Is **this** your lunchbox?
> B: No, **that**'s Joe's lunchbox.
>
> A: Are **these** your socks?
> B: No, **those** are Dad's socks.

7 Speaking *My things*

> ### Use what you know
>
> Put your things on the teacher's desk. Ask and answer.
>
> A: What's this?
> B: It's Mario's calculator.
> A: What are these?
> C: They're Ana's crisps.

In Step 3 you study
● names of the members of a family
so that you can
● write a description of a family

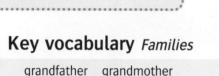
I've got a brother!

1 Key vocabulary *Families*

grandfather grandmother
father mother son daughter
brother sister parent child/children
uncle aunt cousin
husband wife

a ⏱ Complete the sentences with the words in the list. You've got three minutes!

Hi, Robbie. I'm Linda. I'm your mum's sister. I'm your ³ _____ .

Hello, Robbie. I'm your ² _____ , Eric. Pleased to meet you.

I'm Bill, Linda's husband. I'm your ⁴ _____ . And this is our ⁵ _____ , Pete.

Hello, dear. I'm Val. I'm your ¹ *grandmother* .

Hi, Robbie. It's nice to see you. I'm Lucy. I'm your ⁷ _____ .

Hi! I'm your ⁶ _____ .

ROBBIE

🔊 Listen and check.

b Write about Robbie's family.

1 Val is *Robbie's grandmother* .
2 Eric is _____ .
3 Linda is _____ .
4 Bill is _____ .
5 Pete is _____ .
6 Lucy is _____ .

c **Test a friend** Can you make another question like this? Ask and answer your questions.

Who is Lucy's mother's sister's husband?   It's Bill.

2 Reading *A new baby*

a Read the announcement. What's Robbie's surname?

Nick and Zahrah **COOPER** are pleased to announce the birth of

ROBBIE

on 11th November at the Royal Devon and Exeter Hospital.

A brother for Lucy.

b Complete the information.

1 Robbie's birthday is on *11th November* .
2 Lucy hasn't got any _____ , but she's got a _____ .
3 _____ and _____ are Zahrah and Nick's children.
4 _____ is Nick's wife.
5 Zahrah and Nick have got a _____ and a _____ .
6 _____ and _____ are the baby's parents.

3 Writing and speaking *My family*

Use what you know

Imagine you're a member of a famous family. Write a description of your family. Can the class guess who it is?

I've got a brother and a baby sister. My brother's name is Bart ...

Or

Write a description of your family.

Try this!

A and B are two teachers. B is A's son but A isn't B's father. Who is A?

🔊 **CHAPTER 1**

Two messages for Sophie

July 15th

White Lady Cottage

Hi, Sophie!

I'm here at my new house, White Lady Cottage. Do you want to come?

This place is fantastic. I've got a horse, and I know you like riding. Phone me. My mobile number is 07700 903005.

See you soon,

Seth

Sophie Case is from London. She's a singer.

This morning she's got a strange text message on her mobile phone. But who is it from? There isn't a name or a number.

She's got a letter too. It's from her brother, Seth. He's at his new house near Alderley, in the northwest of England.

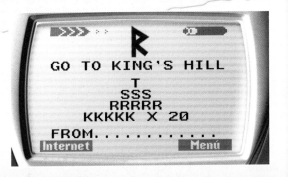

- The sign ᚱ in the text message has got a special meaning. Read the clues and find the meaning. It's a word with seven letters: a '_ _ _ _ _ _ _'.

1. My first letter is in Japan, but not in Panama.
2. My second is in 'a song', but not in 'a singer'.
3. Say 'you'! That's my third letter.
4. My fourth is in 'a car', but not in a Cadillac.
5. My fifth is in 10, but not in 80.
6. My sixth is in 'a name', but not in Naomi.
7. My seventh is in 30, but not in 13.

Extra exercises

1 Look at the family tree and complete the sentences.

1 Emma is Robert and Tom's _mother_ .
2 Angela is David's _____ .
3 Emma is Beth's _____ .
4 David is Beth's _____ .
5 John is Emma's _____ .
6 Robert and Tom are Beth's _____ .
7 Emma is Angela and David's _____ .
8 Emma is Andy's _____ .
9 Andy and Emma are Angela and David's _____ .
10 Angela is Robert and Tom's _____ .

Angela & David

Andy & Alice   Emma & John

Beth   Robert & Tom

2 Choose the right word. 1 b

1 What's 23 x 79?
  I haven't got my _____ .
  a key
  b calculator
  c watch

2 I'm hungry. Have you got any _____ ?
  a tissues
  b crisps
  c badges

3 What's the time? I haven't got my
  _____ .
  a watch
  b CD player
  c mobile

4 I want to phone my parents. Can I use
  your _____ ?
  a message
  b number
  c mobile

5 It's football now. Where are my _____ ?
  a stairs
  b trainers
  c tennis rackets

3 Complete the sentences.

1 It's _Sadie's_ umbrella. (Sadie)
2 _____ lunchbox is in his bag. (Jack)
3 Kate is _____ sister. (Joe and Sadie)
4 _____ tissues are in her pocket. (Lisa)
5 _____ favourite place is Florida.
  (Serena)

4 Complete the sentences with a, some or any.

1 Sadie's got _a_ new CD player.
2 Have you got _____ badges?
3 Emma and John haven't got _____ cousins.
4 Nick and Zahrah have got _____ new baby.
5 Have you got _____ camera?
6 I haven't got _____ magazines.
7 Have Lisa and Sadie got _____ sandwiches?
8 Sadie's got _____ crisps in her bag.

5 Read the text and choose the right word for each space. 1 a

Hi, I'm Gill and this is [1]_____ sister Karen. This is a photo of
[2]_____ mum and dad. [3]_____ teachers. My mum is 35 and
[4]_____ a maths teacher. [5]_____ favourite place is California.
My dad is 38 and [6]_____ an English teacher. [7]_____ favourite
place is Blackpool! [8]_____ favourite people are Karen and me,
of course.

1 a my   b me   5 a Her   b His
2 a we   b our   6 a she's   b he's
3 a They're   b Their   7 a His   b Her
4 a she's   b he's   8 a They   b Their

6 How do you say these sentences in your language?

1 Have you got a pencil?   3 Have a nice day!
  – Yes, here you are.   4 Hurry up!
2 What's the matter?   5 Wait a minute.

Life and culture

Collections

Have you got a collection? What do you collect?

1 Angelika Unverhau from Dinslaken, Germany, has got 168,700 pens. The pens come from 137 countries and they are all different!

3 Suhail Mohammed Al Zarooni, from Dubai, has got 1,500 cars – model cars! He has got police cars, sports cars and limousines. His favourite car is worth a million dollars!

4 John Reznikoff, from Connecticut, USA, has got a very interesting collection – hair! The hair belongs to 115 famous people. John has got some hair from Marilyn Monroe, Einstein and Napoleon.

2 Fiorenzo Barindelli from Lombardy, Italy, has got a collection of 3,677 Swatch watches. His collection is now at the World Museum 2000 in Cesano Maderno, Italy.

5 Steve Fletcher from the UK has got a collection of chewing gum. His collection comes from all around the world. He has got 5,300 different chewing gum packets at his home in London.

ABOUT COLLECTIONS

The British collector Robert Opie recently paid more than £4,000 for two empty matchboxes!

Task

Read about the five different collections, then copy and complete the table.

	1	2	3	4	5
Who	Angelika Unverhau				
Where from	Germany				
What	pens				

4 Descriptions

In Step 1 you study
- adjectives
- *What is/are ... like?*

so that you can
- ask about and describe things

What's it like?

My favourite thing is my dancing lemonade can. It's got arms and legs and it's a very good dancer!
Lee, aged 14.

I've got a new computer game called *The Red Mountain*. It isn't easy, but the graphics and sound are fantastic.
Sadie, aged 12.

New gameplay CD-ROM

My favourite place is Sydney. It's big, noisy and exciting, with a lot of interesting things to do.
Mark, aged 15.

1 Presentation
My favourite things

🔊 Listen and follow the text in your book. Who talks about:

1 an exciting television programme?
2 an interesting city?
3 a good film?
4 a funny possession?
5 a difficult game?

2 Key vocabulary *Adjectives*

a ⏱ Look at the text again. How many adjectives can you find? You've got three minutes!

noisy

b Read the two lists of adjectives. Make pairs of opposites.

big — small

big   happy   noisy   funny   new
good   difficult   great   exciting

easy   serious   bad   small   boring
sad   quiet   old   awful

🔊 Listen and check.

c If you have time, make more pairs of opposites.

3 Key grammar
Position of adjectives

Complete the explanation with *before* or *after*.

> Sky surfing is a **dangerous** sport.
> Sydney is a **big**, **noisy** city.
>
> *In English, adjectives go* _____ *the noun.*

Ⓖ➤ 22c

4 Practice

Write at least two adjectives that you can use with these words.

1 *a funny film, an awful film*

1 a film
2 a place
3 a computer game
4 a book
5 an idea
6 a person

5 Speaking

a 🔊 Listen and follow in your book. Then practise the conversation.

A: What's Lee's favourite thing?
B: His dancing lemonade can.
A: What's it like?
B: It's got arms and legs. It's a very good dancer.

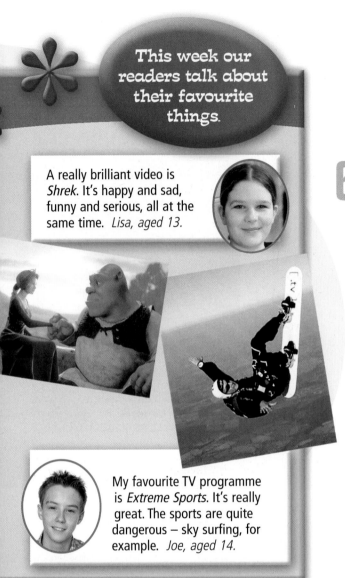

This week our readers talk about their favourite things.

A really brilliant video is *Shrek*. It's happy and sad, funny and serious, all at the same time. *Lisa, aged 13.*

My favourite TV programme is *Extreme Sports*. It's really great. The sports are quite dangerous – sky surfing, for example. *Joe, aged 14.*

Remember!

What's it **like**?
It's got arms and legs.

What's Lisa **like**?
She's great.

What are the beaches **like** in Australia?
They're fantastic.

We use What + is/are + *subject* + like?
to ask for a description.

b Make conversations about Sadie, Mark, Lisa and Joe.

A: What's Mark's favourite place?
B: Sydney.
A: What's it like?
B: It's big, noisy and exciting.

c **What about you?** Ask a friend about his/her favourite things.

possession   film   book   place

A: What's your favourite possession?
B: My new mountain bike.
A: What's it like?
B: It's red and silver.

6 Reading *Mark's 'Happiness recipe'*

a Read Mark's 'Happiness recipe'. How many different ingredients are in the recipe? Are the instructions difficult?

Happiness Recipe

Ingredients:
a sunny day
a quiet beach
a can of lemonade
some Westlife CDs
some good friends
an exciting book
my new surfboard

Instructions:
Mix well. Enjoy your day.

b Read the text again. Do you think it's a good recipe?

7 Writing *My 'Happiness recipe'*

Use what you know

What's your idea of happiness? Make a list of ingredients and write a 'Happiness recipe'.

Ingredients:
Instructions:

Try this!
It's got four legs but it hasn't got any arms.
It isn't an animal.
What is it?

In Step 2 you study
- adjectives
- *has got*

so that you can
- talk about a person's appearance and personality

Dr Jekyll

Mr Hyde

1 Presentation
He's got a cruel face

Read the text. Then match sentences 1–12 with the pictures.

The Strange Case of Dr Jekyll and Mr Hyde is a book by Robert Louis Stevenson (written in 1886). Doctor Jekyll is a scientist. He has got a special potion and, when he drinks the potion, he changes into a different person. He becomes Mr Hyde.

Dr Jekyll: 2 , ...
Mr Hyde: 1, ...

① He's got long, dark hair.

② He's a nice person.

③ He's got straight hair.

④ He's tall.

⑤ He's got a cruel face and his teeth are black.

⑥ He's a kind, honest man.

⑦ He hasn't got glasses.

⑧ He's got brown eyes.

⑨ He hasn't got a friendly face.

⑩ He's a dangerous man. Everyone is scared of him.

⑪ He's got curly hair.

⑫ He's got short, fair hair.

🔊 Listen and check.

2 Key vocabulary
Appearance and personality

a 🔊 Listen and say the words.

long dark tall cruel
black nice dangerous
short straight friendly
honest kind brown
curly fair

Make four lists with these adjectives.

Hair
long

Eyes
brown

Height
tall

Personality
friendly

b Say at least two things about:

1 Dr Jekyll's personality.

2 Mr Hyde's appearance.

3 Listening and speaking

a 🔊 **What about you?** Listen to ten descriptions. Are they true for you? For each sentence, write *true* or *false*.

b Say at least three things about you.

I haven't got blue eyes.

4 Key grammar has got

Complete the short answers.

He's		glasses.
He **hasn't**	**got**	a friendly face.
Has he		straight hair?

Yes, he _____ . / No, he _____ .

G→ 10c

5 Practice

a Make true sentences. Use *has/hasn't got*.

1 *Sadie has got glasses.*

1 Sadie / glasses	4 Joe / curly hair
2 Jack / glasses	5 Lee / blue eyes
3 Lisa / dark hair	6 Sadie / long hair

b **Test a friend** Think of Dr Jekyll or Mr Hyde. Your friend asks questions.

A: Has he got glasses?
B: No, he hasn't.
A: Mr Hyde!
B: Yes. Your turn.

Remember!

He's a nice person. = **He is** a nice person.
He's got short hair. = **He has** got short hair.

6 Speaking

Make at least one sentence for each picture.

1 *She's got a long nose.*

7 Key pronunciation /h/

🔊 Listen and repeat the sentences. Practise the /h/ sound and the links between the words.

Has Anna got a hamster in her anorak pocket?
How many hearts has an octopus got?

Do you know the answer to the second question?

8 Writing and speaking
Guess who!

Use what you know

Think of a well-known person and write a short description.

She's American. She's a singer and she's very famous. She's got long dark hair.

Read your description to a friend. Can your friend guess who the person is?

STEP 3

In Step 3 you study
- parts of the body
- adjectives describing how you feel
- *have got + a headache / a cold*

so that you can
- say how you feel
- write a description of an imaginary person

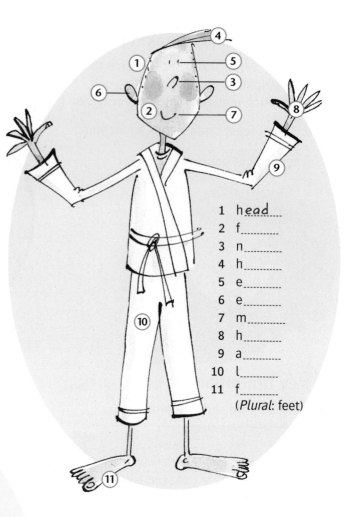

1 h**ead**
2 f
3 n
4 h
5 e
6 e
7 m
8 h
9 a
10 l
11 f
(*Plural:* feet)

1 Key vocabulary *Your body*

arm ear eye face foot hair hand head
leg mouth nose

Look at the picture and complete the words. You've got three minutes!

Listen and check.

2 Key vocabulary *How are you?*

How are you today? Choose a picture for you.

a I'm tired. b I'm fine. c I'm fed up.

d I've got a cold. e I've got a headache. f I've got a stomach ache.

3 Key pronunciation *Stress and intonation*

a Listen to the stress patterns. Then match the sentences in Exercise 2 with the stress patterns.

1 ●● I'm fine.   4 ●●●●●●
2 ●●●   5 ●●●●●
3 ●●●   6 ●●●●

b Listen and check. Repeat the sentences.

c **What about you?** Work with a friend and ask and answer.

How are you today?   I've got a cold.

4 Listening *Song*

a Listen to the song. Is the singer happy or sad?

b Listen again. Then complete the sentences with the adjectives.

black blue red white empty heavy

1 I've got __red__ eyes.
2 My face is _____ .
3 I've got a _____ heart.
4 The day is _____ .
5 My mood is _____ .
6 My arms are _____ .

5 Writing *A 'SuperMe'!*

Use what you know

Write a description of a 'SuperYou'! Use *I've got* + possessive *'s.*

I've got David Beckham's feet.
I've got Picasso's hands.

CHAPTER 2

Sophie's dream

Sophie is at her brother's house. She's tired after her journey from London. She's in bed. She's having a dream.

In her dream she's in a small room. On the wall there's a picture of a woman with long, fair hair and a white dress. There's a black dog with strange yellow eyes in the picture too. The woman is speaking:

'Sophie. I am your guide – not here, but in another world. The dog is your friend too ...'

———— •• ————

The next morning Seth and Sophie are in the garden.

'Seth, why is the cottage called "White Lady Cottage"?'

'Look at the wall near the door. Can you see a woman in the stone?'

'Oh, yes. Who is she?'

'The White Lady. People say she's a messenger from another world! Talk to Mr Neil. His house is near here. I think he knows the story of the White Lady.'

'Has Mr Neil got a dog?'

'Yes, he has. Why?'

'I'm interested. What's the dog like?'

'Er, it's black and it's quite big. It's got very strange eyes … Sophie, what's the matter? Are you OK?'

'Er … yes. Don't worry. I'm fine.'

● Find the meaning of **F**, the sign in the picture. Follow these instructions.

1 Write the word MEANING.
2 Change the Ns to Ss.
3 Put the A after the second S.
4 Change the I to E.
5 Move one of the letters to the end of the word.
   A '_ _ _ _ _ _ _'

● What's the dog called? Complete the five sentences and write the words in the puzzle. Then find the dog's name in the coloured squares.

1 Your eyes, your nose and your mouth are on your ....
2 Your mother and father are your ....
3 44, 13, 16, 27 are ....
4 Everest is a ....
5 The opposite of 'straight' hair is '............' hair.

1		A					
	2			R			
3		U					
4					I		
5		R					

Extra exercises

1 Make questions with *have got* or *has got*.

1 *Has Dr Jekyll got glasses?*

1 Dr Jekyll / glasses ?
2 Lee / blue eyes ?
3 you / a stomach ache ?
4 you / straight hair ?
5 Sadie / a new computer game ?
6 you / a favourite thing ?
7 Jack / a friendly face ?
8 Mr Hyde / a big nose ?

Now answer the questions.

1 *Yes, he has.*

2 Choose the right word. *1 c*

1 I haven't got straight hair. It's _____ .
   a friendly
   b tall
   c curly

2 A: What's that book like?
   B: It's really _____ .
   a sunny
   b exciting
   c quiet

3 Sydney is big and _____ .
   a noisy
   b kind
   c straight

4 My favourite place is _____ .
   a my computer game
   b my bike
   c my room

5 James has got a _____ face.
   a difficult
   b friendly
   c short

6 My favourite thing is _____ .
   a my surfboard
   b my sister
   c my teacher

3 Complete the conversations. *1 a*

1 What's it like?
   a It's funny.
   b Yes, it has.
   c Crisps and peanuts.

2 How are you today?
   a I'm Val.
   b I'm 12.
   c I'm fed up.

3 Has she got glasses?
   a Yes, they are.
   b Yes, she has.
   c Yes, it is.

4 He's got a friendly face.
   a Yes, he's a nice person.
   b He's got a headache.
   c No, it hasn't.

5 I've got a new computer game.
   a How are you?
   b What's it like?
   c Are they exciting?

4 Complete the conversation between Paul and Rod. *1 d*

PAUL: Have you got a favourite thing?
ROD: ¹_____
PAUL: What is it?
ROD: ²_____
PAUL: Has it got any legs?
ROD: ³_____
PAUL: How many arms has it got?
ROD: ⁴_____
PAUL: Is it a good dancer?
ROD: ⁵_____

a A dancing lemonade can!

b Yes, it is. And it's really funny!

c Yes, it's got three legs.

d Yes, I have.

e Two. And it's got glasses.

5 What does the *'s* mean in these sentences?

a is   b has   c possessive *'s*

1 b

1 Our English teacher's got a hamster in her bag.
2 What's the hamster's name?
3 It's called Esmeralda.
4 The hamster's got some peanuts.
5 The hamster's eyes are yellow.
6 It's brown and white.
7 It's eighteen months old.

6 How do you say these sentences in your language?

1 Enjoy your day.
2 What's Lisa like?
3 I'm fed up.
4 It's very exciting.
5 I've got a cold.

Extra reading

London

Do you know the names of any famous places in London?

Every year, 20 million tourists go to London. They visit the famous sights, the museums and art galleries, the shops and theatres.

1

2

Perhaps you prefer the cinema? At the London IMAX (it means 'image maximum') Cinema you can meet a dinosaur and travel to other planets.

3

At Madame Tussauds, you can meet Madonna, David and Victoria Beckham and all your favourite stars!

4

And if you want to see the city from the sky, then go on the London Eye. The view is amazing!

5

If you're interested in animals, then go to London Zoo. If you like science, then visit the Science Museum. There are hundreds of interesting things to see and do.

Task
Think of places in your country.
Write the name of:
1 your capital city.
2 a famous sight there.
3 a famous shop.
4 a famous museum.

About London
Visitors to London often travel on 'the Tube' – the underground train. There are 13 different lines and 300 stations.

Module 2 Review

Language summary

1 have got

We use *have/has got* to talk about

- our possessions
- our appearance
- our family.

Affirmative

I've You've He's/She's/It's We've You've They've	got	a Japanese car. very big feet. five sisters.
I've got = I have got		he's got = he has got

Negative

I/You/We/They	haven't	got a key.
He/She/It	hasn't	
haven't = have not		hasn't = has not

Questions

Have I/you/we/they Has he/she/it	got a key?
Yes, I/you/we/they have. Yes, he/she/it has.	No, I/you/we/they haven't. No, he/she/it hasn't.

What have I/you/we/they What's he/she/it	got?

Check that you can

- use the different forms of *have got*.

Make true sentences.

1 Sadie's cousin Mark .... a surfboard.
2 I .... a bike.
3 Joe .... a brother.
4 The Kellys .... a dog and a tortoise.
5 We .... a hamster.
6 I .... a dictionary.
7 Jack .... any brothers or sisters.
8 Joe and Sadie .... some cousins in Australia.

Now ask your friends:

> Has Mark got a surfboard? Have you ... ?

2 a/an or some

We use *a* before a consonant (for example: b, c, d, t), *an* before a vowel (a, e, i, o, u), and *some* before plural nouns.

I've got	a tortoise called Lightning. an interesting game. some tickets for the concert.

Check that you can

- use *a, an* and *some*.

Make a collection of things, then cover them. How many can you remember? Make a list.

some keys, an umbrella, two mobile phones ...

3 some/any

We use *some* in affirmative sentences, and *any* in negative sentences and questions.

Affirmative
Andy's got **some** crisps.

Negative
He hasn't got **any** peanuts.

Questions
Has he got **any** sandwiches?

Check that you can

- use *some* and *any*.

Complete the conversation.

A: Have you got .... red socks?
B: No, I haven't. Why?
A: I need .... socks for the football match on Saturday.
B: Sorry. I haven't got .... football socks. Ask Joe.

4 Possessive adjectives

In English, possessive adjectives 'agree with' the 'possessor':
You and *your* cousin. *Joe* and *his* sisters. *Sadie* and *her* brother. *Joe* and *Sadie* and *their* parents.

I	➜	my	it	➜	its
you	➜	your	we	➜	our
he	➜	his	you	➜	your
she	➜	her	they	➜	their

Check that you can

- say that something belongs to someone. How do you say these sentences in your language?

1 I like your socks.
2 Robbie is her son.
3 Bill is their uncle.
4 Have you got my address?
5 Do you know our telephone number?
6 Mike is his dad and Sadie is his sister.
7 Nick and Zahrah are her parents.

5 Possessive 's

Joe's bike = the bike belongs to Joe.

> I like Joe's bike.
> Lucy's baby brother is called Robbie.

Check that you can

- use the possessive 's.

Describe these people.

1 Lisa is Sadie's best friend.

1 Lisa is / Sadie ....
2 Sue Kelly is / Joe and Sadie ....
3 Nick and Zahrah are / Robbie ....
4 Robbie is / Lucy ....
5 Kate is / Sadie ....

6 this/that/these/those

We use *this/that* with singular nouns and *these/those* with plural nouns.

We use *this/these* for people or things that are near and *that/those* for people or things that are further away.

> This is my aunt.
> These are my cousins.

> That's my uncle.
> Those are my parents.

Check that you can

- use *this, that, these* and *those*.

Complete the sentences.

What's .... ?

What are .... ?

.... are my trainers! And .... 's my baseball cap!

7 Adjectives

In English, adjectives always have the same form. They go before the noun.

| Herbie is a | very small | animal. |
| Hamsters are | friendly quiet | animals. |

Check that you can

- use adjectives and nouns together.

Put the words in the right order.

1 It's a very difficult game.

1 game / it's / difficult / a / very
2 city / is / very / London / big / a
3 hair / got / he's / curly
4 a / is / man / Mr Hyde / dangerous
5 new / got / watch / I've / a

8 Describing appearance *What's he like?*

We use the expression *What's he/she/it like?* to ask for a description.

| What | 's he/she are they | like? |

| He's | got | brown eyes. |
| They've | | fair hair. |

Check that you can

- describe someone's appearance.

What can you say about the painting?

Vocabulary

Things
anorak
badge
bag
baseball cap
bike
calculator
CD player
key
lunchbox
mobile (phone)
pencil case
socks
tennis racket
tissues
trainers
umbrella
watch

Members of a family
aunt
baby
brother
child (*pl.* children)
cousin
daughter
father (dad)
grandfather (granddad)
grandmother (gran)
husband
mother (mum)
parents
sister
son
uncle
wife

Parts of the body
arm
ear
eye
face
foot (*pl.* feet)
hair
hand
head
heart
leg
mouth
nose
stomach
tooth (*pl.* teeth)

Adjectives
awful
bad
big
boring
cruel
curly
dangerous
dark
difficult
easy
exciting
fair
friendly
funny
good
great
happy
honest
interesting
kind
long
new
nice
noisy
old
quiet
sad
serious
short
small
straight
tall

How you feel
I'm fed up.
I'm tired.
I've got a cold.
I've got a headache.
I've got a stomach ache.

Expressions
Come on!
Have a nice day.
Here you are.
Hurry up!
It's nice to see you.
Pleased to meet you.
Wait a minute.
What's it like?
What's the matter?

Study skills 2   Using a dictionary

1 A dictionary can help you with:

spelling
pronunciation
part of speech (n = noun)
meaning

● When you use a dictionary, you need to know the order of letters in the alphabet. Say these letters and words in alphabetical order.

1 M G S L E H A
2 key quiet pencil case uncle bad
3 tennis tall tissues teacher
4 strange shop straight scientist

2 Be careful! Certain words have two or three meanings:

> Can I use your dictionary? (Can *is a verb.*)
> A can of lemonade. (Can *is a noun.*)
> *And* the can can *is a dance!*

● Do you know the two meanings of the word *mouse*?

3 In certain words the first letter is 'silent'. How do you say these words?

honest know wrong

How's it going?

● **Your rating**

Look again at pages 44–45. For each section give yourself a star rating:

Good ☆ ☆ ☆   Not bad ☆ ☆   I can't remember much ☆

● **Vocabulary**

Choose two titles in the Vocabulary list, then close your book. How many words can you remember for each topic?

● **Test a friend**

Look again at Units 3 and 4. Think of at least two questions, then ask a friend.

> What does 'curly' mean? What's Mr Hyde like?

● **Write to your teacher**

Write a short letter to your teacher in your own language. Say how things are going. Have you got any problems?

● **Your Workbook**

Complete the Learning diaries for Units 3 and 4.

Coursework 2 – All about me!

Read about Jack. Then write about your favourite people, possessions, places, books, films or animals. Use drawings, pictures and photos too.

Important things to me

My favourite place is Manchester. It's a big city in the north of England. My cousin Matt lives there. The Museum of Science and Industry is very interesting.

My favourite possession is my new bag. It's blue, yellow and red. It's got three pockets and two zips. It was a birthday present from my gran.

Badgers are my favourite animals. They're black, white and grey. They've got long bodies and short legs.

My favourite film star is Shrek! He's got a green face and very strange ears.

My best friend is Ben Wilson. He's quite tall. He's got brown eyes and short, dark hair. I like Ben because he's funny, and he's really kind and friendly.

Module 3

Daily life

In Module 3 you study

Grammar

- Present simple
- Revision of question forms
- *Wh*– questions
- Present simple + frequency adverbs
- The verb *have*

Vocabulary

- Names of scary things
- Names of food, drink and meals
- Things people eat in the UK
- Telling the time
- Daily routines

so that you can

- Describe things you do at home and at school
- Write about teenagers in your country
- Talk about fears, likes and dislikes
- Make a conversation about everyday life
- Talk about habits
- Talk about things you eat and drink
- Write a report about food in your country
- Describe daily routines

The Silent Powers

Chapter 3 – The house in the trees
Chapter 4 – The White Lady

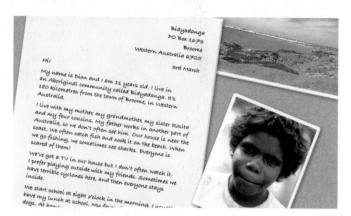

Life and culture

Schools
My name is Dion

Coursework 3

A day in my life
You write about a typical day.

What's it about?

What can you say about the pictures?

Now match the pictures with sentences 1–5.

1 Does she like heights?
2 Do you believe in ghosts?
3 Snakes never blink.
4 Can I ask you some questions?
5 She gets up at half past five.

5 My world

STEP 1

In Step 1 you study
- present simple: affirmative and negative

so that you can
- describe things you do at home and at school
- write about teenagers in your country

1 Key vocabulary *Things you do*

a 🔊 Look at the pictures. Listen and say the words. Then make sentences about things you do regularly.

I use a computer, I wear trainers and I go to a swimming club.

b Think of other things you do regularly.

I play volleyball.

1 read magazines   2 watch TV

3 play the piano   4 wear trainers   5 use a computer

6 eat a lot of crisps   7 drink coffee   8 go to a swimming club

2 Presentation *I go to a judo club*

a 🔊 Listen to Sadie and follow in your book. Who's a computer addict?

SADIE: Joe and I have got the same parents. We live in the same house. We both like music and we're in the same band. But we're different in a lot of ways.

Joe's good at history and maths. I prefer French and art. Joe's favourite TV programme is *Extreme Sports*. I don't watch sport on TV, but I play hockey and I go to a judo club. Joe plays football and basketball.

I write a lot of emails, I use the Internet and I like computer games. My mum says I'm a computer addict! Joe doesn't use the computer every day. He prefers his bike. He reads horror stories too.

I'm a vegetarian, so I don't eat meat. Joe's favourite meal is steak and chips. He doesn't like vegetables. But we both love tomato ketchup. We put it on nearly everything!

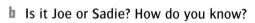

b Is it Joe or Sadie? How do you know?

1 *It's Joe, because he plays basketball.*

①
②

③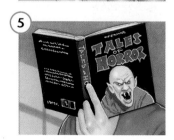
④

⑤
⑥

c Complete the sentences with *Joe, Sadie* or *Joe and Sadie*.

1 .... likes French and art.
2 .... like music.
3 .... doesn't watch *Extreme Sports*.
4 .... goes to a judo club.
5 .... uses her computer every day.
6 .... don't like the same food.
7 .... eats meat.
8 .... like tomato ketchup.

3 Key grammar

Present simple: affirmative and negative

Complete the table.

I/You/We/They Joe/He/She	play ....s	football.
I/You/We/They Sadie/He/She	don't .... doesn't play	the guitar.

G ➔ 5a, b, e

4 Practice

a Make true sentences. Use the correct form of *like*.

1 Sadie doesn't like meat.

1 Sadie / meat   4 I / sport
2 I / vegetables   5 Sadie / steak
3 Joe / basketball   6 Joe and Sadie / music

b Test a friend Write at least one sentence about a student in the class. Read it out. Your friend says 'True' or 'False'.

> Carlos doesn't watch TV.

> False! He watches TV every day!

5 Key pronunciation *Verbs + /s/ /z/ /ɪz/*

🔊 Listen and repeat the verbs.

1 /s/   eats   drinks   likes   writes
2 /z/   reads   plays   lives   goes
3 /ɪz/   uses   watches   changes

6 Writing and speaking

a What about you? Write at least three sentences about things that you do or don't do.

I go to a computer club. I listen to music, but I don't play a musical instrument.

b Work with a friend and compare your lists. Then tell the class.

> We're the same. We don't drink coffee.

> We're different. Maria plays a lot of sport. I don't like sport.

7 Reading

British teenagers

a Read these facts about a typical British teenager. Are you the same or different?

A typical British teenager

- watches a lot of TV.
- wears a school uniform.
- doesn't like homework.
- listens to Radio 1.
- doesn't listen to adults.
- eats a lot of crisps.
- loves tomato ketchup.
- doesn't speak foreign languages very well.

b Make at least two true sentences about you.

I don't wear a school uniform.

8 Writing and speaking

Teenagers in my country

Use what you know

Write about a typical teenager in your country. Make a list like the one in 7a.

A typical teenager in ...
• doesn't wear a school uniform.

Talk about your ideas with the class. Have you got the same ideas?

In Step 2 you study

- present simple: questions and short answers
- names of scary things

so that you can

- talk about fears, likes and dislikes

1 Presentation *Do you like heights?*

a 🔊 Read about Blackpool Tower. Then listen to the conversation with the girl in the photo. Is she all right?

Blackpool is a holiday town in the north of England. Every year a million tourists visit Blackpool Tower. It's got a glass floor 117 metres above the ground. It's called the 'Walk of Faith'.

b 🔊 Listen again, and match the questions with the answers (a–c).

1 Is she scared?
2 Does she want to walk across?
3 Does she like heights?

a Yes, she does. But she's too scared.
b No, she doesn't.
c Yes, she is. She's terrified.

c Now imagine you're at the 'Walk of Faith' and answer the questions.

1 Are you scared?
  a Yes, I am. I'm terrified.
  b Yes, I'm quite scared.
  c No, I'm not. It's fantastic!

2 Do you want to walk across?
  a No, I don't.
  b Yes, I do. But I'm too scared.
  c Yes, I do.

3 Do you like heights?
  a No, I don't.
  b It depends.
  c Yes, I do.

2 Key grammar *Present simple: questions and short answers*

Complete the short answers. Then complete the explanation.

| Do Does | you he/she | like heights? | Yes, I do. Yes, he/she .... No, I .... No, he/she doesn't. |

We make questions with do *or* .... *+ subject + verb.*

G → 5c, f

3 Practice

a What can you remember about Joe and Sadie in Step 1? Make questions.

1 *Does Sadie like tomato ketchup?*

1 Sadie / like tomato ketchup ?
2 Sadie / watch sport on TV ?
3 Sadie / eat meat ?
4 Joe / like vegetables ?
5 Joe / read horror stories ?

b Ask and answer the questions in 3a.

Does Sadie like tomato ketchup?   Yes, she does.

4 Speaking

a **What about you?** Work with a friend and ask and answer at least two questions.

> Do you read horror stories?
>> No, I don't.

b If you have time, think of other questions with *Do you ...?*

Do you — like / watch / read — horror films? / magazines? / sport? / comics? / funny films? / horror stories?

5 Key vocabulary *Scary things*

🕐 Match the words with the numbers in the picture. You've got two minutes!

spider shark the dark alien UFO
thunder bat rat vampire ghost

🔊 Listen and check.

6 Listening *Song*

a 🔊 Listen to the song. Choose a title.

  a Spiders b Scared c Horror stories

b 🔊 Listen again. Complete these sentences from the song.

1 .... you scared of spiders?
2 .... you believe in aliens?
3 Are you .... of sharks?
4 Do you .... in vampires?

c Ask and answer other questions. Use the words in Exercise 5.

A: Do you believe in ghosts?
B: No, I don't.
A: Are you scared of the dark?
B: Yes, I am.

7 Writing and speaking *A questionnaire*

Use what you know

Choose at least two topics from the list. Write a questionnaire and interview your friends.

books comics magazines films sport
computer games

	Yes	No
Do you read books?	✓	
What's your favourite book?	*Ghost from the Sea*	
Do you like music?	✓	
Who's your favourite singer?	*Craig David*	

Try this!
It lives in hot countries. It eats insects.
It doesn't attack people, but they're scared when
they see it. It's got eight legs. It begins
with *t* and ends with *a*. What is it?

STEP 3

In Step 3 you study
• question forms (revision)
• present simple: *Wh-* questions
so that you can
• write a conversation about everyday life

1 Presentation *Where do you come from?*

Match the questions with the answers (a–h).

1 Do you speak English?

2 Where do you come from?

3 Have you got a family?

4 Why are you here?

5 What do you want?

6 Are you all right?

7 Do you want a drink?

8 What sort of food do you eat?

a Yes, please.

b Because I'm on holiday.

c No, I'm not. I'm fed up.

d I like fruit. Have you got any bananas?

e I'm from another planet.

f Yes, I have.

g I want to meet the Queen.

h Yes, I do.

Listen and check. Practise the questions and answers.

2 Key grammar *Wh- questions*

Complete the table with *What, Who, Why* and *Where*.

....		live?
....	do you/they	want?
....	does he/she	want to meet?
....		want to meet the Queen?

3 Practice

Make questions.

1 *Where does the alien come from?*

1 Where / the alien / come from ?
2 What sort of food / aliens / like ?
3 What / they / drink ?
4 Who / the alien / want to meet ?
5 Why / he / want to visit our planet ?
6 Where / the Queen / live ?
7 When / the Queen / eat her lunch ?

4 Key pronunciation
Stress and intonation

Listen to the sentences. Then match the sentences with the stress and intonation patterns.

1 Where do you live?
2 Do you live in a flat?
3 What do you eat?
4 Do you like burgers?

a ●●●●●● ➚

b ●●●● ➚

c ●●●●● ➚

Listen again and repeat the sentences.

5 Writing and speaking
An interview

Use what you know

Work with a friend. Imagine that one of you is someone famous. Write at least three questions and answers about your life.

A: What sort of TV programmes do you watch?
B: I watch a lot of sport.

Read your conversation to another pair of students.

G ➤ 14

CHAPTER 3

The house in the trees

Sophie is in the wood near White Lady Cottage. But it's late and she doesn't know where she is. There's a house in the trees. An old man is at the door. Perhaps he can help her.

'Come in, Sophie.'

'You know my name!'

'Yes. You're Sophie Case, Seth Case's sister. You're nineteen. Your birthday is on 12th June. You live in London. You're a singer. You play the piano and you've got a cat called Henry. Is that correct?'

'Yes, it is. But how do you know? Who are you?'

The old man is silent, but his eyes are friendly. Sophie has got the text message in her pocket.

'Is this text message from you?'

'That isn't important, Sophie. Look! I've got something for you.'

In his hand he's got a small white stone.

'This is a moonstone. It's got special powers. Use it when things are difficult. Go home now … Cabal, go with Sophie to White Lady Cottage!'

At the door there's a big black dog with strange yellow eyes. It's the dog in Sophie's dream.

GO TO KING'S HILL
T
S S S
R R R R R
K K K K K ×20

- When Sophie sees the black dog, she knows who the old man is. What's the man's name?

- Find the meaning of **X**, the sign on the moonstone. The answer is in the mirror.
  A '__ __ __ __'. What does the word mean?

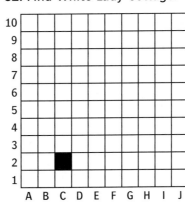

- The old man's house is on square C2. Find White Lady Cottage. Which square is it?

  1 Go one square west.
  2 Go three squares north.
  3 Go one square northwest.
  4 Go two squares northeast.
  5 Go one square north.
  6 Go one square northeast.
  7 Go three squares east.
  8 Go one square south.
  9 Go one square southeast.
  10 Go one square southwest.

Extra exercises

1 Choose the right word.

1 My brother _____ like vegetables.
  a doesn't
  b don't
  c do

2 Sharks _____ in the sea.
  a lives
  b live
  c doesn't live

3 _____ Joe watch sports programmes on TV?
  a Is
  b Does
  c Don't

4 _____ you like chips?
  a Do
  b Does
  c Are

5 Andy _____ tomato ketchup on everything.
  a put
  b don't put
  c puts

6 Andy and Alice _____ in aliens.
  a believes
  b doesn't believe
  c believe

2 Complete the conversations.

1 Are you scared of the dark?
  a No, I don't.
  b No, I'm not.
  c Yes, I do.

2 Are you all right?
  a Yes, he's OK.
  b No, it's wrong.
  c No, I'm fed up.

3 What does he like?
  a He's got brown hair.
  b He's fine, thanks.
  c Tomato ketchup.

4 Do you like horror stories?
  a Yes, I like it.
  b Yes, I do.
  c Yes, I am.

5 Does Joe write a lot of emails?
  a No, he doesn't.
  b Yes, she does.
  c Yes, he is.

3 Match the questions in A with the answers in B.

A

1 Do you believe in ghosts?
2 Are you scared of thunder?
3 What's your favourite book?
4 Where does she come from?
5 What sort of programmes do you watch?
6 What sports does she play at school?

B

a *Ghost from the Sea.*
b Madrid. She's Spanish.
c Hockey and football.
d Yes, I am. I'm terrified.
e It depends – sport, films.
f No, I don't.

4 Match the verbs and nouns.

1 f *live in a flat*

1 live   a two foreign languages
2 listen   b hockey
3 read   c a uniform
4 write   d in UFOs
5 play   e coffee
6 believe   f in a flat
7 speak   g English magazines
8 wear   h to music
9 drink   i emails

5 Complete the conversations.

1 A: Where _____ you come from?
  B: Madrid.

2 A: What languages do you _____ ?
  B: English and French.

3 A: _____ she like meat?
  B: No, she doesn't. She prefers vegetables.

4 A: When do you _____ to the swimming club?
  B: On Saturday.

5 A: _____ are you here?
  B: Because I'm on holiday.

6 A: _____ do you live?
  B: In a flat.

6 How do you say these sentences in your language?

1 Are you all right?
2 It depends.
3 What sort of books do you like?
4 Where do you come from?
5 We both like music.
6 I'm a computer addict.

Extra reading

Schools

What time do you start school in the morning? What's your favourite subject?

The UK

Children go to school from Monday to Friday. They start school at the age of four or five and they leave at 16 or 18. When they are 11, they go to a secondary school. Lessons start at about 9 am and finish at about 3.30 pm. Pupils eat lunch in the canteen or take their own 'packed lunch'. When school finishes, some children go to clubs, for example, music or computer clubs.

Australia

Children begin school at the age of five. At the age of 11, they go to a High School for six years. Some students go to a special type of high school, for example, Agricultural High Schools and Sports High Schools. Australia is a very big country so, in some areas, there aren't any schools and pupils study at home. The 'School of the Air' started in Alice Springs, in the desert. Pupils listen to their lessons on the radio, and today they use computers and emails too.

The USA

Children start elementary school at six. When they are 12, they go to a Junior High School. At 15, pupils change to a Senior High School where they can choose what they want to study. They usually stay there for three years. At the end of their final year, they have a big party. It's called 'the senior prom'.

ABOUT SCHOOL

The Latin name for school is *ludus*. It means 'play'!

Task

Are these sentences true or false?

1 Children in the UK can leave school at 16.
2 Pupils in the UK have their lunch at home.
3 Australian teenagers all go to the same sort of school.
4 In some parts of Australia there aren't any schools.
5 American children start school when they're four.
6 American students go to the senior prom when they're 15.

6 I'm usually late!

STEP 1

In Step 1 you study
- present simple + frequency adverbs

so that you can
- talk about habits

1 Presentation *Snakes never blink*

a Match the sentences with the photos.

1 Dolphins always live in groups.
2 Tarantulas usually live in a hole in the ground.
3 Bears often eat fish.
4 Giraffes sometimes clean their ears with their tongues.
5 Snakes never blink.

🔊 Listen and check.

b How do you say these words in your language?

- always
- usually
- often
- sometimes
- never

c Are these sentences true or false? Can you guess?

1 Dolphins always sleep with one eye open.
2 Snakes usually live in the sea.
3 Gorillas don't usually drink water.
4 Lions aren't usually very energetic.
5 Tarantulas often attack people.
6 Dolphins never kill sharks.
7 Snakes kill 40,000 people every year.
8 Bears sometimes eat spiders.

2 Key grammar *Position of frequency adverbs*

Complete the explanation with *before* or *after*.

> Bears **often** eat fish.
> They don't **often** attack people.
> Do they **often** eat other animals?
>
> Dolphins are **usually** very intelligent.
> They aren't **usually** dangerous.
> Are they **usually** friendly?
>
> *Frequency adverbs generally go* _____ *the main verb.*
> *But they go* _____ *the verb be.*

 G 23

3 Practice

a **What about you?** Make true sentences with *always, usually, often, sometimes* or *never*.

1 *I usually sleep for about nine hours.*

1 I sleep for about nine hours.
2 I eat fish.
3 I drink water.
4 I'm very energetic.
5 I'm bored.

b If you have time, make more sentences about your habits.

I often use the Internet.

c **Test a friend** Choose a sentence from Exercise 1. Write the words in the wrong order. Ask a friend to say the right sentence.

groups / live / dolphins / in / always

4 Reading and listening

A questionnaire

a Read the questionnaire. Who is it for?

a a child   b a teenager   c an adult

b Listen to Ben and write his answers to the questionnaire. Then talk about Ben's habits.

> He usually does his homework on time.

c **What about you?** Write your answers to the questionnaire.

Good habits? Bad habits?

Choose the best description for you!

1 Homework
 a I always do my homework on time.
 b I usually do my homework on time.
 c I don't usually do my homework on time.

2 Your room
 a I always tidy my room at the weekend.
 b I sometimes tidy my room.
 c I never tidy my room.

3 Housework
 a I often help with the housework.
 b I sometimes help at home.
 c I never do any housework.

4 TV
 a I always watch TV when I get home.
 b I sometimes watch TV in the evening.
 c We haven't got a television.

5 On time?
 a I'm often late.
 b I'm sometimes late.
 c I'm not usually late.

6 Exercise
 a I play a lot of sport and I walk a lot.
 b I do PE at school but that's all.
 c I'm lazy. I don't often get any exercise.

5 Speaking

a Read the questions and think of your answers.

What are you like? Are you:

a telly addict?   lazy?   energetic?

helpful?   well-organised?

b Ask a friend at least two questions.

A: Are you lazy?
B: It depends. I don't often tidy my room.
A: Are you well-organised?
B: Sometimes. But I'm usually late.

6 Writing *My habits*

Use what you know

Write about your good habits and your bad habits.

I've got a lot of bad habits.
I don't often help at home.

I've got some good habits too.
I'm usually on time.

STEP 2

In Step 2 you study
- names of food, drink and meals
- the verb *have*
- things people eat in the UK

so that you can
- talk about things you eat and drink
- write a report about food in your country

1 Key vocabulary *Food and drink*

a Look at the pictures. How many words do you know?

1 bread   2 toast   3 butter   4 cereal

5 milk   6 tea   7 coffee   8 orange juice   9 water

10 eggs   11 yoghurt   12 cheese

13 ham   14 chicken   15 sausages   16 fish

17 fruit   18 vegetables   19 salad   20 pasta   21 sandwich

Listen and say the words.

b What about you?
Make true sentences about things you eat and drink.

I like salad but I don't like vegetables.
I never eat yoghurt.

2 Key pronunciation
Vowel sounds

a Listen to the rhythm drill, then join in.

A: What's for breakfast?
B: Toast, eggs, milk and tea.
A: What's for lunch?
B: Chicken, bread, juice and salad.
A: What's for dinner?
B: Pasta, fish, fruit and cheese. Are you hungry?
A: Yes, I am.
B: You're always hungry!

b Find 'food' words in the drill with the same vowel sounds as these words.

1 big – milk, chicken, ...

1 big   4 ten
2 go   5 you
3 see   6 bat

Listen and check.

Try this!

How many 'food and drink' words can you make using these letters?

TBOMRUCHNEASIFDSLKG

3 Reading and listening *A survey about food*

a 🔊 Close your book and listen to the conversation. Which meals do they talk about?

It's Saturday morning. Joe is in the town centre. A Japanese student called Tamiko is talking to him.

TAMIKO: Excuse me. Is this seat free?

JOE: Yes, it is.

TAMIKO: Can I ask you some questions? It's a survey about English food.

JOE: Oh, I see! Er, what do you want to know?

TAMIKO: What do you usually have for breakfast?

JOE: Er, well, it depends. I usually have ¹t_____ and ²f_____ j_____ . I sometimes have ³c_____ .

TAMIKO: What about lunch?

JOE: I sometimes have ⁴s_____ , and I sometimes go to the school canteen. I have ⁵p_____, or a ⁶b_____ .

TAMIKO: And what do you have for dinner?

JOE: Well, my sister doesn't eat ⁷m_____, so we often have ⁸p_____ . I sometimes have ⁹m_____ with ¹⁰v_____ , or ¹¹f_____ . And I usually have a snack when I get home from school – you know, a packet of ¹²c_____ , something like that.

TAMIKO: What's your favourite meal?

JOE: That's easy. ¹³S_____ and ¹⁴c_____ .

TAMIKO: That's all. Thank you very much.

JOE: You're welcome.

b 🔊 Listen again. Complete the 'food' words in the conversation.

4 Reading *Tamiko's report*

Read Tamiko's report and check your answers to 3b.

Food in the UK
I interviewed Joe Kelly. He's 14 and he lives in Exeter. He has toast or cereal for breakfast, and fruit juice. At lunchtime, he sometimes has sandwiches, or he eats in the school canteen. He has pizza or a burger. He usually has a snack when he gets home from school, for example a packet of crisps. For dinner he has pasta, or meat and vegetables, or fish.

Joe's favourite meal is steak and chips. But not all British people eat meat. 12% of people in the UK are vegetarian.

Some popular meals in the UK are: curry (that's Indian), spaghetti bolognese (that's Italian), pizza (that's Italian too), chilli con carne (that's Mexican), and fish and chips (that's English!).

5 Speaking

What about you? Ask and answer questions about your meals.

> What do you usually have for breakfast?

> I usually have toast and orange juice.

6 Writing *Food in my country*

Use what you know

Write a short report about things you eat, and some popular meals in your country.

Title: Food in …
Paragraph 1: I usually have … for breakfast. At lunchtime I … . When I get home from school … . In the evening I …
Paragraph 2: Some popular meals in my country are …

In Step 3 you study
- telling the time
- vocabulary for daily routines

so that you can
- say when you do things

1 Key vocabulary
The time

a ⏱ Put the clock times in the right order. Write: 2.00 2.15 ... You've got five minutes!

five past three
ten past four
quarter past two
twenty past three
twenty-five past two
two o'clock
half past four
twenty-five to five
twenty to four
quarter to three
five o'clock
ten to four
five to five

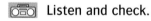 Listen and check.

b Draw at least three clocks and ask a friend *What's the time?*

What's the time?

It's half past ten.

2 Key vocabulary *Daily routines*

a Look at the pictures of Kitty's day. Then match the pictures with the sentences.

Kitty Jordan is only 14 but she's a junior British Diving Champion. She trains every day.

 a
 b
 c
 d
 e
 f
 g
 h
 i

1 She gets up.
2 She goes to the swimming pool.
3 She has a shower.
4 She leaves the swimming pool.
5 She catches the bus.
6 She gets to school.
7 She gets home.
8 She has her dinner.
9 She goes to bed.

b Guess what time Kitty does these things.

1 *I think she gets up at six o'clock.*

3 Listening *Kitty's Day*

a 📻 Listen to Kitty. Look at the sentences in 2a and write the correct times. 1 5.30

b Work with a friend. Check your answers.

What time does Kitty get up?

She gets up at half past five.

4 Speaking *My routines*

Use what you know

Ask a friend at least three questions about his or her day.

What time do you get up?

I usually get up at quarter past seven.

CHAPTER 4

The White Lady

Sophie is talking to Seth about Mr Neil.

'Seth, that old man knows my name, my age, my birthday and my cat's name!'

'Don't worry. He's a bit strange, but he's always very kind.'

'His dog's strange too. It understands everything he says.'

'Listen. Don't worry about Mr Neil and his dog. Come and have dinner. Do you want to go riding tomorrow? You can ride my horse. She's called Epona.'

'That's great! Thanks.'

———— ●●● ————

After dinner, Sophie is in her room. She's got the moonstone in her hand.

Suddenly there's a strange white light in the room, and there's a woman near the window.

'The White Lady! What do you want?'

'Don't be scared, Sophie. We need your help.'

'Why me?'

'Because your name is in the Book of Signs. When the Silent Powers choose a person, they always write the name in the Book. Your mission is important, Sophie. But don't talk about it with other people. Go to the Circle of Seven at eleven o'clock tomorrow. Remember! The Circle of Seven, in Hunter's Wood.'

- Find the meaning of **ᚲ**, the sign in the light from the moonstone. Use the letters in this circle of seven.

Other people don't know about Sophie's mission. It's '__ __ __ __ __ __ __'.

Extra exercises

1 Read the descriptions. Complete the names of the animals.

1 They always live in groups and are usually very intelligent. d_____
2 They never blink. s_____
3 They clean their ears with their tongues. g_____
4 They usually live in a hole in the ground. t_____
5 They like fish and they sometimes eat other animals. b_____

2 Write complete sentences.

1 *Sadie and Joe usually have breakfast at 7.30.*

1 Sadie and Joe have breakfast. (*usually / at 7.30*)
2 I listen to the radio. (*never / in the afternoon*)
3 We have chicken and chips. (*always / on Saturday*)
4 My grandmother goes to the cinema. (*sometimes / at the weekend*)
5 Ben is late for school. (*often / in the morning*)
6 My brother has a shower. (*never / in the morning*)
7 I'm hungry. (*always / at eleven o'clock*)

3 Make questions. Use *you*.

1 *What time do you get up?*

1 what time / get up ?
2 what / usually / have for breakfast ?
3 what time / go to school ?
4 when / usually / finish school ?
5 what / do in the evening ?
6 what time / usually / go to bed ?

Now answer the questions.

4 Complete the conversation.

A: Excuse me, is this seat free?
B: 1 _____
A: Can I ask you some questions?
B: 2 _____
A: What do you do after school?
B: 3 _____
A: Do you watch TV in the evenings?
B: 4 _____
A: What's your favourite programme?
B: 5 _____
A: When do you watch that?
B: 6 _____

a Sometimes, but not every day.

b I usually play on my computer.

c *The Simpsons.*

d Yes, it is.

e On Monday and Wednesday.

f Yes, of course.

5 Choose the right word.

1 I often help my parents with the _____ .
   a homework
   b home
   c housework
2 My best friend plays a lot of sport. She's very _____ .
   a energetic
   b helpful
   c lazy
3 I usually have a _____ at lunchtime.
   a sausages
   b sandwich
   c cereal
4 We sometimes _____ steak and chips for dinner.
   a have got
   b has
   c have
5 Kitty always _____ at half past five.
   a get up
   b doesn't get up
   c gets up

6 How do you say these sentences in your language?

1 Is this seat free?
2 Thanks very much.
   – You're welcome.
3 Excuse me. Can I ask you some questions?
4 I have a snack at lunchtime. That's all.
5 Are you a telly-addict?

Extra reading

My name is Dion

Have you got a pen friend?
Where does your pen friend live?

Bidyadanga
PO Box 1673
Broome
Western Australia 6725

3rd March

Hi!

My name is Dion and I am 11 years old. I live in an Aboriginal community called Bidyadanga. It's 180 kilometres from the town of Broome, in Western Australia.

I live with my mother, my grandmother, my sister Rosita and my four cousins. My father works in another part of Australia, so we don't often see him. Our house is near the coast. We often catch fish and cook it on the beach. When we go fishing, we sometimes see sharks. Everyone is scared of them!

We've got a TV in our house but I don't often watch it. I prefer playing outside with my friends. Sometimes we have terrible cyclones here, and then everyone stays inside.

We start school at eight o'clock in the morning. I usually have my lunch at school. My favourite school meal is hot dogs. At home my favourite meals are chicken soup and egg on toast.

Write to me soon.

Your friend,

Dion

ABOUT ABORIGINALS
The people in Dion's community are from five Aboriginal groups. The different groups each speak their own language, and they speak English too.

Task
Read the letter from Dion and answer the questions.
1 Where does Dion live?
2 Does he live in a big town?
3 Does his father work in Bidyadanga?
4 Do Dion and his family always have their meals in the house?
5 Does he often watch TV?
6 Where does he usually play?
7 What time does he start school?
8 What's his favourite school meal?

Module 3 Review

Language summary

1 Present simple

We use the present simple to describe 'things that are generally true'.

Affirmative

I/You/We/They	eat octopus. like sharks.
He/She/It	likes sharks. eats octopus.

Don't forget! Verb + s/es after he/she it.
See Spelling notes, page 142.

Negative

I/You/We/They He/She/It	don't doesn't	like spiders. eat meat.
don't = do not	doesn't = does not	

Questions and short answers

Do Does	you/they he/she	like sport? eat meat?
Yes, I/we/they do. No, I/we/they don't. Yes, he/she does. No, he/she doesn't.		

What Where When	do	you they	want? live? get up?
Who Why	does	he she	like? forget everything?

Check that you can

1.1 ● describe people's habits and routines.

Put the words in the right order and make sentences.

1 and / live / Exeter / Mel / in / Barney
2 o'clock / up / seven / I / get / at
3 to / goes / a / Sadie / club / judo
4 crisps / lot / we / a / eat / of
5 TV / watch / they / evening / every
6 teeth / every / I / day / clean / my

1.2 ● use the present simple with verb + s/es.

Change *I* to *My friend Buzz* and rewrite the sentences.

1 *My friend Buzz reads a lot of ghost stories.*
1 I read a lot of ghost stories.
2 I walk to school.
3 I do my homework before dinner.
4 I watch *Friends* on TV.
5 I help with the housework.
6 I play the guitar.

1.3 ● make negative sentences with *don't* or *doesn't*.

1 Sadie and Lisa _____ like maths.
2 Ben _____ drink coffee.
3 Lee _____ believe in ghosts.
4 Jack _____ like heights.
5 I _____ want to do this exercise!

1.4 ● make questions and answers with *do, does, don't* and *doesn't.*

1 _____ Joe play a lot of sport? – Yes, he _____ .
2 _____ you wear glasses? – Yes , I _____ .
3 Where _____ Mel and Barney go to school?
   – In Exeter.
4 _____ Lee do his homework on time?
   – No, he _____ .
5 _____ you get a lot of exercise? – Yes, I _____ .
6 When _____ Kitty get up? – At half past five.

2 Frequency adverbs

Frequency adverbs describe how 'frequently' we do things. They go before the main verb but after the verb *be*.

They	always often usually sometimes never	walk to school.

I'm He's/She's/It's You're/We're/They're	always often usually sometimes never	late.

Check that you can

● use *always, often*, etc.

What do you talk about with your friends? Use the frequency adverbs in the box above and make a true sentence for each topic in the list.

We often talk about sport.

sport   food   parents   clothes   films   music

3 Telling the time

one o'clock
five past one
ten past one
quarter past one / one fifteen
twenty past one
twenty-five past one
half past one / one thirty
twenty-five to two
twenty to two
quarter to two / one forty-five
ten to two
five to two

Check that you can

● talk about the time.

Match these times with words in the list above. Which one isn't in the list?

1.40   1.10   1.30   5.01   1.55
1.15   1.45   1.20

4 like + noun

We don't use *the* in these sentences:

| I like | peanuts. |
| He doesn't like | chicken. |

Check that you can

● say what you like and don't like. Make true sentences about the things in the pictures.

I like bats. I don't like football.

5 have got or have?

We use *have* (and not *have got*) to describe 'actions'.
We have: *a meal, a bath, a shower, some coffee, a sandwich.*

| What time **do** you **have** your breakfast? |
| I **don't have** a bath every day. |
| He **has** a shower every morning. |
| We usually **have** sandwiches for lunch. |

| I've got some crisps in my bag. |
| He's got a new computer. |

Check that you can

● use *have* and *have got* correctly.

Complete the sentences with *have/has* or *have got / has got*.

1 Joe always _____ a shower after a football match.
2 I know! I _____ the answer!
3 Sadie _____ a brother and a sister.
4 I usually _____ my lunch in the canteen.
5 My granddad _____ a bath every Friday night.
6 Are you hungry? I _____ some apples in my bag.

6 Expressions of time

in	the morning
	the afternoon
	the evening
	the summer
	July
on	Saturday
	3rd April
at	night
	the weekend
	the end of the lesson
	ten o'clock
	lunchtime

Check that you can

● describe when you do things.

Work with a friend. Make questions and give true answers.

When do you clean your teeth?

In the morning and in the evening.

When do you	clean your teeth?
	do your homework?
	tidy your room?
	go to the computer club?
	play football?

Vocabulary

Activities and routines

to catch (the bus)
to clean
to do (my homework)
to drink
to eat
to get (to ...)
to get up
to go
to have (a shower/ a meal)
to help
to leave
to listen (to ...)
to play (hockey/ the piano)
to read
to sleep
to tidy
to use
to visit
to walk
to watch
to wear

Likes and dislikes

bat
comic
(the) dark
ghost
history
hockey
horror film
Internet
judo
maths
rat
science fiction
shark
spider
thunder

Food and drink

bread
burger
butter
cereal
cheese
chicken
chips
coffee
curry
egg
fish
fruit
ham
meat
milk
orange juice
pasta
pizza
salad
sandwich
sausage
spaghetti
steak
tea
toast
vegetable
water
yoghurt

meal
snack

breakfast
dinner
lunch

Expressions

Are you all right?
Excuse me.
I see.
It depends.
That's all.
What sort of ... ?
What's the time?
You're welcome.

Study skills 3 How do you learn?

1 Think about the things you do in your English lessons. For each activity, write your opinion: *fine*, *not bad*, or *awful*.

1 not bad

1 acting conversations
2 learning new words
3 listening to the cassette/CD
4 reading

5 singing
6 speaking in class
7 talking about grammar
8 writing

Share your ideas with the class.

2 Do you do any of these things outside school? Make true sentences with *always*, *sometimes*, *never*, etc.

I sometimes watch films in English.

I watch films in English.
I read English or American magazines.
I read web pages in English.
I write emails in English.
I listen to songs in English.
I write letters to a pen friend in English.

Share your ideas with the class.

How's it going?

- ## Your rating

Look again at pages 66–67. For each section give yourself a star rating:

Good ☆ ☆ ☆   Not bad ☆ ☆   I can't remember much ☆

- ## Vocabulary

Choose two titles in the Vocabulary list, then close your book. How many words can you remember for each topic?

- ## Test a friend

Look again at Units 5 and 6. Think of at least two questions, then ask a friend.

> Where's Blackpool? What's Joe's favourite meal?

- ## Write to your teacher

Write a short letter to your teacher in your own language. Say how things are going. Have you got any problems?

- ## Your Workbook

Complete the Learning diaries for Units 5 and 6.

Coursework 3 – All about me!

Read about Jack. Then describe your typical day. For example, write about:
- the beginning of your day
- how you get to school
- your school timetable
- the end of the day.

Use drawings, pictures and photos too.

A day in my life

Good morning!

On a school day, my day begins at quarter past seven. I have breakfast with my mum. She leaves the house before me because she starts work at eight. She's a nurse.

AS 09865
Student
Bus Pass

VALID FROM 01 SEP

NAME
JACK ELLIS

SCHOOL
WESTOVER SCHOOL

Issued subject to conditions – see over

I usually go to school by bus. I catch the number 97 in St. David's Hill. I often walk to the bus stop with Sadie. This is my school bus pass.

This is my school timetable for Monday.

MONDAY	
8.55	Registration
9.10	Maths
10.10	PE
11.10	Break
11.30	Biology
12.30	Lunch
1.20	Registration
1.30	History
2.30	English

Our lessons finish at 3.30.

6pm	6.0 News (419) (T)	6.0 The Simpsons (758099) (T) (R)	6.0 London Tonight (815) (T)
	6.30 Regional News Programmes (159)	6.20 The Fresh Prince Of Bel-Air (752815) (T) (R)	6.30 News (167) (T)
7pm	7.0 This Is Your Life Another life story. (9896) (T)	6.45 Buffy The Vampire Slayer Xander bumps into his future-self. (244273) (T)	7.0 Emmerda Debbie heads fo Emily's horror. (4
	PICK 7.30 EastEnders Billy thinks Den's back. (985) (T) ● See Today's Picks	7.30 The Good Life Vintage laughs with the Goods. (525) (T) (R)	7.30 First E The property

WWF®

I get home at about ten past four. In the evening I do my homework and I watch TV. I sometimes play computer games and I write emails. I often write emails to people in my Wildlife Watch Group, and I look at the World Wildlife website.

Module 4

Inside and outside

In Module 4 you study

Grammar

- *There is/are*
- Uncountable nouns
- Prepositions
- *Can* for ability and possibility
- *Must/mustn't*
- Imperative

Vocabulary

- Homes
- Names of things in a room
- Food
- Verbs that describe abilities
- Names of places in a town

so that you can

- Describe different homes
- Write a description of your dream home
- Ask questions about places and food
- Invent some 'disgusting recipes'
- Say where things are
- Understand and give a description of a room
- Talk about abilities
- Make a notice for a club
- Talk about things you can do in your town
- Describe the sights and sounds around you
- Tell people what to do!

The Silent Powers

Chapter 5 – The Circle of Seven
Chapter 6 – Devil's Bridge

Life and culture

Homes in the UK
Stephen Hawking

Coursework 4

My neighbourhood
You draw a map of your neighbourhood and describe places near your house.

My neighbourhood

My best friend Ben lives here. There's a park opposite his house.

There's a fish and chip shop at the end of our road. We sometimes have fish and chips for dinner when Mum is busy.

This is our house.

I catch the bus to school here. You can get a bus to the town centre too. In the ... centre there are two ...

What's it about?

What can you say about the pictures?

Now match the pictures with sentences 1–5.

1 She lives on a houseboat.
2 There are some posters on the wall.
3 He can fly!
4 You can go shopping at the shopping centre.
5 You must do your homework.

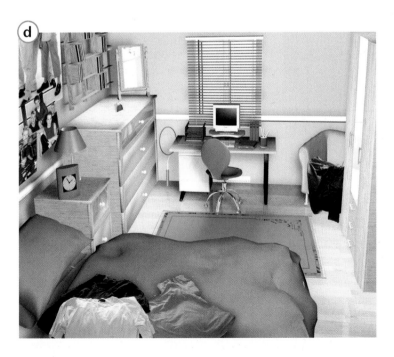

STEP 1

In Step 1 you study
- homes vocabulary
- *There is/are*

so that you can
- describe different homes
- write a description of your dream home

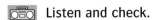 The Kellys' house

1 Key vocabulary *Homes*

Match the words with the numbers in the picture.

1 *upstairs*

living room   bedroom   garden   dining room   hall
shower   kitchen   toilet   upstairs   downstairs   bathroom

🔊 **Listen and check.**

2 Presentation
There are 132 rooms.

Match the photos with the descriptions.

a There are 132 rooms. There's a room called the Oval Office. There's an apartment for the President on the third floor.

b There's a big living room and a kitchen downstairs. There isn't a dining room. There are three bedrooms upstairs.

c There isn't a bathroom, but there's a shower and a toilet. There aren't any bedrooms.

🔊 **Listen and check.**

(2) The White House

(3) A houseboat

3 Key grammar There is/are

Complete the explanation with *there is, there isn't, there are* and *there aren't*.

> There's a living room.
> There **isn't** a dining room.
> There **are** three bedrooms.
> There **aren't** any bedrooms downstairs.
>
> *We use _____ / _____ before a singular noun (a living room).*
> *We use _____ / _____ before a plural noun (three bedrooms).*

G → 11a, b

4 Practice

a **What about you?** Make four sentences about your home.

1 *There's a small kitchen.*

1 There's _____ .   3 There are _____ .
2 There isn't _____ . 4 There aren't _____ .

b **Test a friend** Write a true or false sentence about one of the photos. Read it to a friend.

> There are two bedrooms in the houseboat.

> False! There aren't any bedrooms.

5 Key pronunciation
Stress in sentences

a 🔊 Listen to the poem, then join in.

There's a hill by the sea,
On the hill there's a house.
In the house there's a room
With a small white door.
There's a sign on the door
And the sign says ME.
But the door is locked
And there isn't a key.

b Find the stressed words in the poem.

There's a <u>HILL</u> by the <u>SEA</u>.

6 Writing *My dream home*

Use what you know

Write a description of your dream home. Use *There's* and *There are*.

My dream home is an old house in Jamaica. There are ten bedrooms. There's a big garden and a swimming pool.

Find new words in your dictionary: *gym, tennis court, ...*

> **Try this!**
> Which word is the odd one out? Why?
> living room   bedroom   kitchen
> mushroom   bathroom   dining room

In Step 2 you study
- *Is/Are there … ?* + short answers
- uncountable nouns

so that you can
- ask questions about places and food
- invent some 'disgusting recipes'

1 Presentation *Is there any juice?*

a What can you say about the photos?

b 📻 Close your book and listen to the conversation between Sadie and Kate. What does Sadie want for dinner?

Sadie's sister Kate is a student at Bristol University. She lives on a houseboat on the River Avon. Sadie is visiting her for the weekend.

KATE: Come in, Sadie. This is the kitchen, and this is the living room.

SADIE: What a great place! Is there a television?

KATE: No, there isn't, but I've got a radio.

SADIE: Are there any bedrooms?

KATE: No, there aren't. I sleep in this room. Anyway, sit down. Do you want a drink?

SADIE: Yes, please. I'm really thirsty. Is there any apple juice?

KATE: I'm not sure. Let's see … no, there isn't any fruit juice. Sorry. There's some water.

SADIE: That's fine.

KATE: Here you are.

SADIE: Thanks. I'm hungry. What's for dinner?

KATE: What do you fancy?

SADIE: Er … vegetable lasagne!

KATE: OK, but I haven't got any vegetables, and there isn't any lasagne. Do you want to come to the supermarket?

SADIE: Yes, all right.

KATE: We need some milk, and some cheese too. Can you make a shopping list? There's some paper on the desk.

c 📻 Listen again and follow in your book. Are these sentences true or false? Correct the false sentences.

1 There isn't a radio.
2 There aren't any bedrooms.
3 There's some apple juice.
4 There are some vegetables.
5 There isn't any paper.

d Read the conversation again. Find at least four things for Kate's shopping list.

2 Key grammar
Is/Are there …? + short answers

Complete the questions and short answers.

Is there a radio?	Yes, there _____ .
_____ there a television?	No, there _____ .
Are there any beds?	Yes, there _____ .
_____ there any bedrooms?	No, there _____ .

Ⓖ➤ 11c

3 Practice

Ask and answer questions about things in your classroom. Use *Is there / Are there?*

1 CD player
2 television
3 posters
4 telephone
5 computers
6 cupboards

〔 Is there a CD player? 〕 〔 Yes, there is. 〕

4 Reading and listening
Kate's shopping

a Read the shopping list. Then write the complete list in your notebook.

fruit j............   c............
m............   tomatoes
bread   peppers
l............   onions
water   mushrooms

b 🔊 Listen to Kate and Sadie at the supermarket. Sadie is hungry. What does she want to buy?

c 🔊 Look at your list and listen again. Number the words when you hear them:

onions — 1

What haven't Kate and Sadie got?

5 Key grammar *Uncountable nouns*

Complete the explanation with *some* and *any*.

There are 'countable' nouns and 'uncountable' nouns.

● *Countable nouns can be singular:*

a bottle   an onion

and plural:

some bottles   some onions

● *Uncountable nouns are always singular, but we use* some *and* any *with them:*
There's some water.
There isn't any bread. Is there any cheese?

We use .... *with uncountable nouns in affirmative sentences.*
We use .... *with uncountable nouns in negative sentences and in questions.*

G➤ 18a, b

6 Practice

a Are these nouns countable or uncountable?

sandwich   bread   ham   butter   cheese   pasta   eggs

b Complete the sentences with *a, some* or *any*.

1 Have we got .... ham?
2 I want to make .... sandwich. Is there .... bread?
3 We've got .... butter but we haven't got .... cheese.
4 We need .... pasta and .... eggs.

7 Speaking

a Work with a friend. Practise the conversation.

A: Is there any bread in the trolley?
B: No, there isn't.
A: Are there any peppers?
B: Yes, there are.

b Look at Kate's shopping list again. Ask and answer at least three more questions.

8 Speaking *Disgusting recipes*

Use what you know

Think of a disgusting recipe.
For example:

A milkshake with ice cream and onions.
An omelette with sardines and mushrooms.

Tell the class your idea. Vote for the most disgusting idea.

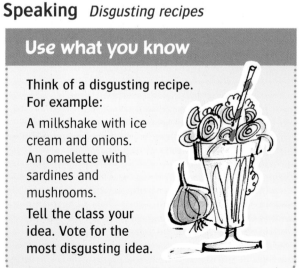

In Step 3 you study
- names of things in a room
- prepositions

so that you can
- say where things are
- understand and give a description of a room

1 Key vocabulary *Things in a room*

Match the words on the plan with the numbers in the picture.

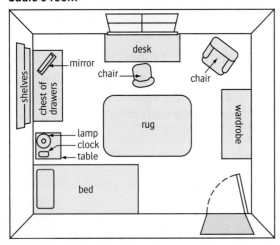

Sadie's room

shelves, mirror, chest of drawers, desk, chair, chair, wardrobe, lamp, clock, table, rug, bed

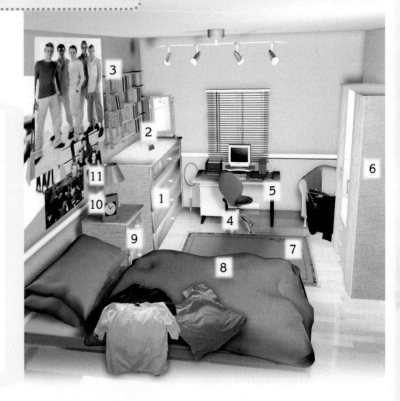

Listen and check.

2 Key grammar *Prepositions*

How do you say these words in your language?

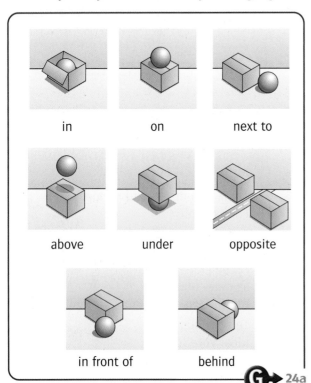

in   on   next to

above   under   opposite

in front of   behind

G→ 24a

3 Practice

Use prepositions from Exercise 2. Complete the description of Sadie's room.

The bed's on the left and there's a small wardrobe on the right. There are some posters ¹_____ the wall ²_____ the bed. There's a table ³_____ the bed, and there's a lamp and a clock ⁴_____ the table. There's a chest of drawers ⁵_____ the table, and there are some shelves ⁶_____ the chest of drawers. There's a desk ⁷_____ the door, ⁸_____ the window. There's a chair in the corner and another chair ⁹_____ the desk. You can see Sadie's tennis racket ¹⁰_____ the desk.

4 Writing and speaking *My room*

Use what you know

Draw a plan of your room and label it. Then work with a friend. Tell your friend at least four things about your room.

> The bed's next to the window.

Can your friend draw a plan of your room?

CHAPTER 5

The Circle of Seven

The next morning at ten to eleven Sophie and Epona are in Hunter's Wood. But Sophie doesn't know where the Circle of Seven is. There are three paths in front of her. Which is the right path? Sophie remembers the moonstone in her pocket. When she touches it, she knows the answer.

'Come on, Epona! This is the right path.'

At the end of the path, there's a circle of seven stones. In the middle of the circle, there's something on the ground. It's a piece of paper with a message.

> YOUR PROGRESS IS GOOD, SOPHIE.
>
> • YOUR NAME IS IN THE BOOK OF SIGNS.
>
> • YOU BELIEVE IN THE POWER OF THE MOONSTONE.
>
> • WE NEED A WHITE HORSE, AND YOU'VE GOT EPONA.
>
> BUT THERE ARE LOTS OF DANGERS. IF YOU MEET THE RED QUEEN, BE CAREFUL!

In the trees behind Sophie, there's a strange red light …

- Which is the right path? These three cards are clues. Is it the path on the left, on the right, or in the middle?

- Find the meaning of **<**, the sign in the tree.

V	G	K	A
N	T	U	H
C	W	P	F
D	Y	E	L
B	S	R	J

The first letter is in the northeast corner, opposite B.

The second letter is under V.

The third letter is next to B, on the right.

The fourth letter is under T.

The fifth letter is above R.

The last letter is next to J, on the left.

When Sophie has got a problem, the moonstone gives her the '_ _ _ _ _ _'.

Extra exercises

1 Complete the questions with *Is* or *Are*.

1 .... there any onions in this lasagne?
2 .... there a shower in the bathroom?
3 .... there any cheese in the recipe?
4 .... there any peppers in Kate's trolley?
5 .... there a rug in your bedroom?
6 .... there any posters in the President's office?

2 Complete the sentences with *a, an, some* or *any*.

1 There are .... tomatoes in the cupboard.
2 Are there .... good films on TV?
3 There isn't .... river in our town.
4 Is there .... ham in this omelette?
5 Is there .... orange umbrella in the hall?
6 There's .... bread on the table in the kitchen.
7 There isn't .... tea or coffee.

3 Complete the conversations.

1 Has the house got a garden?
  a Yes, he has.
  b Yes, it has.
  c Yes, there is.

2 I'm really thirsty.
  a Do you want a sandwich?
  b Do you want a shower?
  c Do you want a drink?

3 Is there any milk?
  a No, there isn't.
  b No, there aren't.
  c No, it isn't.

4 What vegetables do you like?
  a Onions and cheese.
  b Mushrooms and peppers.
  c Tomatoes and sardines.

5 Where's the garden?
  a Behind the house.
  b In the hall.
  c Upstairs.

4 Put the words in the right order and make sentences.

1 some / wall / there / the / on / are / photos
2 desk / the / is / lamp / there / on / a ?
3 White / gym / 's / the / House / a / there / in
4 are / any / shelves / there / Sadie's / in / room ?
5 mirror / there / a / chest / of / drawers / above / 's / the
6 a / there / in / is / wardrobe / bedroom / your ?

5 Read the text and choose the right word for each space.

Kate lives ¹............ a beautiful houseboat on the River Avon. ²............ are two rooms on the boat, a kitchen ³............ a living room. There aren't ⁴............ bedrooms so Kate sleeps in the living room. There isn't a TV on the houseboat but there ⁵............ a radio in the living room and there ⁶............ some books and magazines too.

1 a under	b on	c at
2 a Their	b They	c There
3 a and	b but	c so
4 a some	b a	c any
5 a are	b 's	c isn't
6 a a	b are	c 's

6 Put the words into the right group.

apartment   bathroom   cupboard   living room   houseboat
clock   house   door   flat   hall   chair   rug   kitchen
bed   dining room

Homes	Rooms	Things in a room
apartment		

7 How do you say these sentences in your language?

1 What do you fancy?
2 What have we got? – Let's see.
3 What's for dinner?
4 Anyway, come in and sit down.
5 What a great place!
6 I'm thirsty. Can I have a drink?

Life and culture

Homes in the UK

Look at the photos of different homes in the UK. Are they the same as homes in your country?

Richard and Kerry Jones live in Edinburgh, in Scotland. They've got four children, Patrick, Shona, Dean and Sara. They live in a semi-detached house near the city centre. It's a typical British home. There are three bedrooms and a bathroom upstairs. Downstairs, there's a large living room, a kitchen and a toilet. The house has got a small garden at the front and a big garden at the back. There's also a garage.

Shona is a student in Leeds. She lives in a flat on the 12th floor. It's got one bedroom, a very small kitchen, and a bathroom.

Kerry's parents live in a cottage near the sea. They've got a beautiful garden, two cats and a dog.

Patrick lives in a caravan in the country. It's got a bedroom, a living area with a kitchen, a shower room and a toilet. He sometimes moves from place to place.

ABOUT HOUSES

The British Prime Minister lives at 10 Downing Street. (It's a terraced house in the middle of London.) But the Prime Minister hasn't got a front-door key.

Dean's best friend, Mark, lives in a terraced house in the centre of Edinburgh. It's about 200 years old. The rooms are very big but it hasn't got a garden.

Task

Are these sentences true, false or 'we don't know'?

1 The Jones's house has got two gardens.
2 Shona's flat isn't very big.
3 The bathroom is downstairs in Kerry's parents' cottage.
4 The cottage has got a garage.
5 There isn't a toilet in Patrick's caravan.
6 Mark lives in a modern house.
7 Mark often sits in his garden at the weekend.

8 Having fun

In Step 1 you study	so that you can
• verbs that describe abilities	• talk about abilities
• can/can't	• make a notice for a club

1 Key vocabulary *Abilities*

🕐 Match the words with the pictures. You've got three minutes!

swim   dive   stand on my head
sing   draw   speak Chinese
play the guitar   play football
cook   dance   ski   ride a horse

🔊 Listen and check.

2 Presentation *Yes, I can!*

a This is the first verse of a song. How many abilities are there?

I can swim and I can dive.
I can stand on my head.
I can ride a bike.
I can. Oh yes, I can!

b Look at the words in Exercise 1 and imagine more sentences from the song.

I can ski.

3 Listening *Song*

a 🔊 Listen to the song. The boy in the song has got a problem. What's his problem?

He can't ...

b 🔊 Listen again. Are these sentences true, false or 'we don't know'?

1   He can play the piano.
2   He can dance.
3   He can't cook.
4   He can draw.
5   He can't play tennis.

4 Key grammar can/can't

Complete the short answers.

I/You/He/She/We/They	can	swim. speak Chinese.
Can you/he/she/they		play the guitar? ride a horse?
Yes, No,	I/he/she/we/they	----------- . ----------- .

G ▶ 12a–f

5 Practice

Ask and answer questions about the boy in the song.

A: Can he swim?
B: Yes, he can.
A: Can he play the piano?
B: We don't know. / I can't remember.

6 Speaking

a **What about you?** Work with a friend and ask and answer questions about your abilities.

A: Can you speak Arabic?
B: No, I can't. What about you?
A: Yes, I can. My grandfather's Moroccan.

b Tell the class about your friend.

> Maria can speak Arabic but she can't speak Chinese.

7 Reading *The Champion Birdman*

a Read the newspaper article. What can the Champion Birdman do?

You probably think that people can't fly. Well, you're wrong. Every year in August, there's an International Birdman Competition in Bognor, on the south coast of England. The Champion Birdman can fly 44 metres. There are some fantastic competitors this year. You can see a flying frog, an elephant with very big ears, and a man with wings! There are Birdman competitions in Italy, Holland, Japan, America, Australia and New Zealand too. You can get more information on the Birdman website.

The people in the photos aren't crazy! They're competitors in the International Birdman Competition.

b Read the article again. Then answer the questions.

1 When is the competition?
2 Where is it?
3 What sort of competitors can you see?
4 Are there Birdman competitions in other countries?
5 Is there a Birdman website?

c Answer the questions with *Yes, I can.* or *No, I can't.*

Can you:
1 translate: *frog, wings*?
2 pronounce: *competition*?
3 fly?
4 draw one of the competitors in this year's competition ?

Do numbers 1, 2 and 4 with the class. Don't try to do number 3!

8 Writing *A notice for a club*

Use what you know

Can you sing? Can you act? Can you dance?

Join the **Westover Drama Club!**

● You can get more information on our website:
● www.westoverdrama.org.uk
● Or telephone Jim 01632 965008

Design a notice for a club. Use:

Can you ... ? Join the ... .You can get more information from ...

Try this!
Can they fly?
a mosquito   a plane
a horse   a bat   a bird
a fly   a chicken

In Step 2 you study
● names of places in a town
● *can* for possibility
● *can* + see/hear

so that you can
● talk about things you can do in your town
● describe the sights and sounds around you

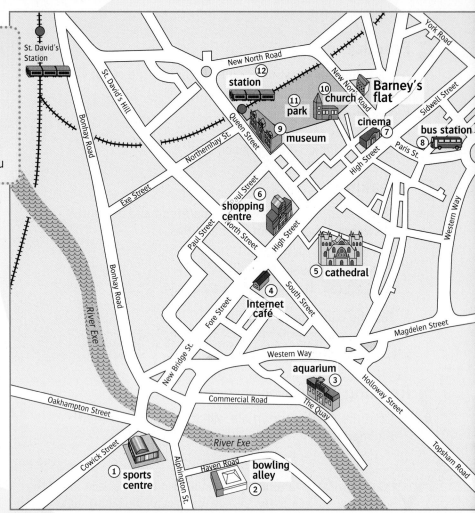

1 Key vocabulary
Places in a town

a Look at the places on the map.

🎧 Listen and say the words.

b Make sentences about places near your school.

There's a sports centre near our school. There isn't a station.

2 Presentation
You can visit the aquarium

a Read the information about Exeter. Is it an interesting town?

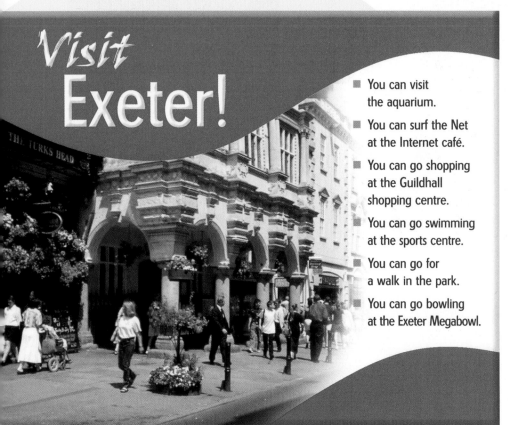

Visit Exeter!

■ You can visit the aquarium.

■ You can surf the Net at the Internet café.

■ You can go shopping at the Guildhall shopping centre.

■ You can go swimming at the sports centre.

■ You can go for a walk in the park.

■ You can go bowling at the Exeter Megabowl.

b Ask and answer the questions. Where can you:

1 buy a CD?
2 meet your friends?
3 get some exercise?
4 write an email?
5 see a shark?
6 find a very old map?

> Where can you buy a CD?

> At the shopping centre.

3 Key grammar
can *for possibility*

How do you say these sentences in your language?

> You can surf the Net.
> You can't visit the museum in the evening.

Ⓖ▶ 12f

4 Practice

a What else can you do in Exeter?
Make at least three sentences.

You can go to the cinema.

b **What about you?** What can/can't you do
in your town? Share your ideas.

> You can play basketball at the sports centre.

> You can't go bowling.

5 Presentation *I can hear the traffic*

a Look again at the map of Exeter. Where does
Barney live? Can you find his flat?

b Close your book and listen to Barney.
What can he see and hear? Can you remember?

He can hear his brother's radio.

c Read the text and check.

BARNEY: When I wake up in the morning,
I can hear my brother's radio. Sometimes I
can hear my mum and dad in the kitchen.
I can hear the traffic in the street outside,
and sometimes I can hear a train. When
I open my eyes, I can see the wardrobe,
and my posters on the wall. When I look
out of the window, I can see the shops
and houses opposite our flat. I can see
some trees and the park behind the shops.

6 Key grammar *can + see/hear*

How do you say these sentences in your language?

> I can hear the traffic outside.
> I can see the park.

G → 12g

7 Practice

a **What about you?** Answer the questions.

1 What can you see and hear when you wake up?
2 What can you see when you look out of your window?

b **Test a friend** Think of something you can see
or hear now. Can your friend guess what it is?

A: I can see something beginning with 'c'.
B: Cupboard.
A: Yes! Your turn!
B: I can hear something beginning with 'd'.

8 Key pronunciation *can/can't*

 Listen and repeat the sentences. Practise
the pronunciation of *can* and *can't*.

1 /kɑːnt/ You **can't** dance in the **park** in the **dark, Mark!**
2 /kæn/ Yes, **Sam,** you **can.**
3 /kən/ **Anita can** swim, she **can** dive, she **can** ski.

9 Writing and speaking *An amazing view*

Use what you know

> What an amazing view!

Imagine you're at the top of a very tall
building in the middle of your town.
Describe the view.

I can see the station.
I can see the sports centre and ...

In Step 3 you study
- *You must/mustn't ...*
- Imperative (revision)

so that you can
- tell people what to do!

1 Presentation *You mustn't argue*

a 🔊 Close your book and listen. Why can't Sadie watch *Top of the Pops*? What's the real reason?

SADIE: Dad, can I watch *Top of the Pops*?

MR KELLY: No, you can't. You must do your homework.

SADIE: I haven't got any homework this evening.

MR KELLY: Well, you must tidy your room. It's in an awful mess.

SADIE: I know! But I can do that after *Top of the Pops*.

MR KELLY: No, you can't. You mustn't go to bed late tonight.

SADIE: But it finishes at eight o'clock. What's the problem?

MR KELLY: I want to watch the football. And don't be rude!

b 🔊 Listen again and follow in your book. Then put the words in the right order and make sentences.
1 your / you / homework / do /must
2 tidy / room / your / must / you
3 go / you / late / mustn't / bed / to
4 rude / be / mustn't / you

2 Key grammar *must/mustn't*

How do you say these sentences in your language?

> You must tidy your room.
> You mustn't go to bed late.

G ➔ 13

3 Practice

a Complete the sentences with *must* or *mustn't*.
1 You _____ be late.
2 You _____ wear an anorak.
3 You _____ have a shower.
4 You _____ be rude.

b **Role play** If you have time, act the conversation between Sadie and her dad.

4 Reading *A poem*

a Read the poem. Who is the writer – an adult or a teenager?

Don't say that!

Why do adults always say ...?
Be quiet.
Don't argue.
Say 'Pardon?', not 'What?'.
That isn't funny.
Don't be silly.
You must wash your hands.
You can't wear that.
Don't interrupt.
That's enough from you.
Why can't adults be more polite?

b Who says these things to you?

Our teacher often says 'Be quiet!'.

> **Remember!**
>
> *We use the imperative to give instructions.*
> *Affirmative:* Be polite. Come here.
> *Negative:* Don't be rude. Don't go.

5 Writing *My poem*

> **Use what you know**
>
> Work with a friend. Write at least two or three lines for another poem.
>
> *Why do adults always say:*
> *You must ... You mustn't ... Don't ...*

CHAPTER 6

Devil's Bridge

Sophie wants to send an email to a friend in London. She's at the computer. Suddenly, there's a message on the screen.

'Seth, where's Devil's Bridge?'

'It's in Hunter's Wood. Follow the river and, after about a kilometre, there's a little bridge. That's Devil's Bridge.'

———— • • • ————

Half an hour later Sophie is at the bridge. On the bridge, in a circle of red light, there's a tall woman with long dark hair.

'I am the Red Queen. Look at me, Sophie!'

Sophie is terrified. When she looks into the Red Queen's eyes, she can't speak and she can't move.

'Your mission is impossible, Sophie. You can't help Mr Neil and his friends. Give me the moonstone and go back to London.'

Sophie has got the moonstone in her hand, but she can hear a voice in her head: 'You mustn't listen to the Red Queen, Sophie. And don't look into her eyes.'

Sophie can feel the power of the moonstone in her hand. When she looks at it, she can speak again.

'The moonstone belongs to me. You can't have it. Go!'

There's a flash of silver light, and Sophie is alone on Devil's Bridge.

- Find the meaning of **N**, the sign on the computer screen. Here are your clues:

Look at the four numbers. Each number is a letter of the alphabet. Can you find the word?

The meeting with the Red Queen is a '20 5 19 20' for Sophie.

Extra exercises

1 Put the letters in the right order and write the places.

1 cinema

1 meacin
2 usb tasiont
3 quaruiam
4 tertenin éafc
5 prak
6 ingpohsp terecn

2 Answer the questions. Use the words in Exercise 1.

1 At the cinema.

1 Where can I see a film?
2 Where can I see a shark?
3 Where can I surf the Net?
4 Where can I go shopping?
5 Where can I catch a bus?
6 Where can I play football?

3 Complete the sentences with *can* and one of the verbs in the list.

speak   swim   use   play   cook   ride   see

1 *Can* you *speak* French?
2 _____ you _____ a computer?
3 _____ Andy _____ the guitar?
4 _____ you _____ a horse?
5 _____ you _____ 100 metres?
6 _____ Joe _____ lasagne?
7 _____ you _____ the park from your flat?

4 Match the replies with the questions in Exercise 3.

a Yes, I can. I do my homework on it every day.
b No, I can't, but I can see the school.
c No, but he can play the piano.
d No, I can't. I don't like animals.
e Yes, and German.
f Yes, he can. He's very interested in cooking.
g Yes, I can. I go to the swimming pool every week.

5 Choose the right word.

1 He can swim but he _____ dive.
   a can't   b isn't   c doesn't
2 Can you _____ on your head?
   a fly   b swim   c stand
3 You can catch the 92 at the _____ opposite the school.
   a trees   b bus station   c website
4 Sadie, look at the time! You _____ go to bed.
   a don't   b mustn't   c must
5 Joe and Sadie live at number 18. That's _____ house.
   a their   b they're   c there

6 Match the beginnings with the endings and make sentences.

1 c You must tidy your desk.

1 You must tidy   a to the doctor.
2 You must go   b silly.
3 You musn't put   c your desk.
4 You mustn't be   d your socks.
5 You mustn't argue   e your shoes on the table.
6 You must wash   f with everyone.

7 Complete the sentences with the words in the list.

wash   be   close   tidy   go

1 _____ quiet! Westlife are on the radio.
2 _____ the window! It's cold in here.
3 Look at your hands – go and _____ them!
4 Sadie, _____ your room. It's in an awful mess.
5 It's late, Joe. _____ to bed.

8 How do you say these sentences in your language?

1 It's an amazing view.
2 My room's in a mess.
3 Don't be silly!
4 Be quiet. That's enough.
5 Do you want to go swimming?

Extra reading

Stephen Hawking

Look at the photo of Stephen Hawking.
What do you think he can and can't do?

Stephen Hawking is a famous British scientist. He is often on TV and in magazines. He lives in Cambridge. He is married and has got three children.

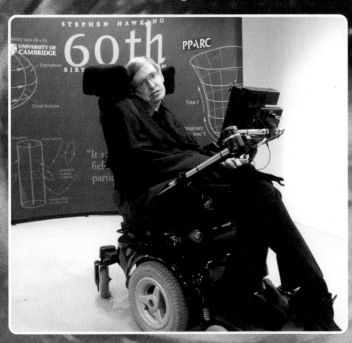

Stephen has got a neuromuscular disease: he can't move and he can't talk. A nurse helps him to dress, eat and wash. She is with him 24 hours a day. He can communicate with other people with a special computer. He uses this computer to teach at the University of Cambridge, where he is a professor of mathematics. He has got a special wheelchair with a portable computer.

You can sometimes see him in the streets and shops of Cambridge. He loves shopping – especially buying clothes for his daughter.

Stephen is an ambitious and determined man. He can't write so he dictates his ideas to a secretary. He is the author of a best-selling book called *A Brief History of Time*. It is about the beginning of the world and other cosmic mysteries.

ABOUT STEPHEN HAWKING

Stephen once appeared on *The Simpsons* and talked to Homer about the universe.

Task

Answer the questions.

1 Where does Stephen Hawking come from?
2 Why can't he move or talk?
3 Why has he got a nurse?
4 What does he use to communicate?
5 What does he teach?
6 How does he write his books?

Module 4 Review

Language summary

1 There is/are

We use *there is* with singular nouns and *there are* with plural nouns. In a list, we use *there is* if the first noun is singular: *There's a gym, some tennis courts and a swimming pool.*

	Singular	Plural
Affirmative	There's a cinema near our school.	There are three cinemas.
Negative	There isn't a park.	There aren't any parks.
Questions and answers	Is there a river? Yes, there is. No, there isn't.	Are there any rivers? Yes, there are. No, there aren't.

Check that you can

1.1 ● describe places near your home.

Make true sentences with *There is/isn't/are/aren't*.

There's a café near my home.
There aren't any cinemas.

1 shopping centre   4 tennis courts
2 bus station   5 station
3 supermarkets   6 Internet cafés

1.2 ● ask and answer questions with *Is/Are there ...?*

Complete the questions, then ask and answer.

> Are there any lakes near our town?

>> Yes, there are. / No, there aren't.

1 .... any lakes near our town?
2 .... a town called Alice Springs in Australia?
3 .... any mountains in Italy?
4 .... a cathedral in Exeter?
5 .... any volcanoes in England?
6 .... a river in the middle of our town?

Make more questions if you have time.

2 Countable and uncountable nouns

We can count *cars* and *dogs*. These are called 'countable' nouns. They can be singular: *a car*, or plural: *some cars*.

a car   some cars

We can't count *butter* or *music*. These are called 'uncountable nouns'. They haven't got a plural form.

butter   music

Check that you can

● understand the difference between singular, plural and uncountable nouns. Put the words in the right list.

bread   egg   sandwiches   apple   pasta   cheese
onions   coffee   milk   vegetables   fruit   sausage
orange juice   bananas   omelette   chips   water

Singular *There's a/an ...*	Plural *There are some ...*	Uncountable *There's some ...*
egg	sandwiches	bread

Sometimes nouns can be countable or uncountable.

a yoghurt   some yoghurt

3 Prepositions of place

Prepositions of place answer the question *Where is it?*.

in   on   above   under   behind   in front of next to   opposite   in the middle   in the corner on the right   on the left   by

Check that you can

● use prepositions of place.

Make six true sentences about things in your classroom or things at home. Use the prepositions in the box.

4 can

We use *can/can't*:

- to describe abilities: *I can ride a bike but I can't ride a horse.*
- to describe possibility: *We can ride our bikes by the river.*
- to ask for permission: *Can I ride your bike, please?*

We also use it with the verbs *see* and *hear*:
I can't see Sam. Can you hear that music?

Affirmative and negative

I/You/He/She/We/They	can can't	swim well. swim in the lake. sit here.
can't = cannot		

Questions and answers

Can	I/you/he/she/we/they	go to the cinema tonight? play basketball?
Yes, I/you/he/she/we/they can. No, I/you/he/she/we/they can't.		

Check that you can

4.1 ● talk about abilities.

What can/can't these animals and people do?

Bears can't fly.

1 bears   2 a small baby   3 dolphins   4 birds

4.2 ● talk about possibilities.

Imagine that you wake up one morning and you're only 10 centimetres tall.
What is and isn't possible?

I can't go to school!

4.3 ● ask for permission.

Make questions using pairs of words from the lists.

Can I sit here, please?

watch   sit   have   go   play

a sandwich   your guitar   to Jack's house   TV   here

5 must

We use *must* and *mustn't* when we talk about obligation and orders.

Affirmative and negative

I/You/He/She/We/They	must mustn't	go now. tell Sadie.
mustn't = must not		

Check that you can

- use *must* and *mustn't*.

Complete the sentences.

1 You _____ clean your teeth every day.
2 It starts at 7.30. We _____ be late.
3 Close your eyes! You _____ look.
4 Look at the time. I _____ go.
5 It's my CD player and you _____ use it.

6 there, they're and their

They've all got the same sound!
Be careful!

> Joe and Sadie aren't here.
> **They're** late.
> Have you got **their** telephone number?
> **There's** a message on my mobile.

Check that you can

- use the three different forms correctly.

Complete the sentences.

1 Joe and Sadie live at number 18. Look! That's _____ house.
2 I can see them. _____ in the garden.
3 _____'s a dog in the garden too. That's Sam.

7 Imperative

We use the imperative for instructions and orders:

Affirmative	*Negative*
Close your eyes!	Don't look!
Be quiet!	Don't be silly!

Check that you can

- tell people what to do!

Make four sentences.

Don't be	to this song.
Come	in front of me.
Listen	to the cinema with us.
Don't sit	rude.

Vocabulary

Homes
apartment
flat
house
houseboat

bathroom
bedroom
dining room
garden
kitchen
living room
shower
toilet

door
floor
room
stairs
wall
window

downstairs
upstairs
(first) floor

Things in a room
bed
chair
chest of drawers
clock
cupboard
desk
lamp
mirror
photo
poster
radio
rug
shelf/shelves
table
television
wardrobe

Places in a town
aquarium
bowling alley
bus station
cathedral
church
cinema
gym
Internet café
museum
park
shop
shopping centre
sports centre
station
street
supermarket
swimming pool
tennis court

Activities
to go bowling
to go shopping
to go swimming
to go for a walk
to surf the Net

Abilities
to cook
to dance
to dive
to draw
to fly
to play (football / the guitar)
to ride (a bike / a horse)
to sing
to ski
to speak (Chinese)
to stand on your head
to swim

Expressions
Anyway, ...
Be quiet!
Come in.
Let's see.
That's enough.
What do you fancy?
What's for dinner?
Yes, all right.

Study skills 4 Learning vocabulary

To help you remember new words, you can:

1 put them in groups

2 use translation

3 use pictures

Choose six words from the vocabulary list and write them in your notebook. Use 1, 2 or 3 to help you remember them.

How's it going?

● Your rating

Look again at pages 88–89. For each section give yourself a star rating:
Good ☆ ☆ ☆   Not bad ☆ ☆   I can't remember much ☆

● Vocabulary

Choose two titles in the Vocabulary list, then close your book. How many words can you remember for each topic?

● Test a friend

Look again at Units 7 and 8. Think of at least two questions, then ask a friend.

> Is there a desk in Sadie's room?
> What does 'That's enough!' mean?

● Write to your teacher

Write a short letter to your teacher in your own language. Say how things are going. Have you got any problems?

● Your Workbook

Complete the Learning diaries for Units 7 and 8.

Coursework 4 – All about me!

Read about Jack. Then draw a map of your neighbourhood. Describe some of the places near your home and the things you do there.

My neighbourhood

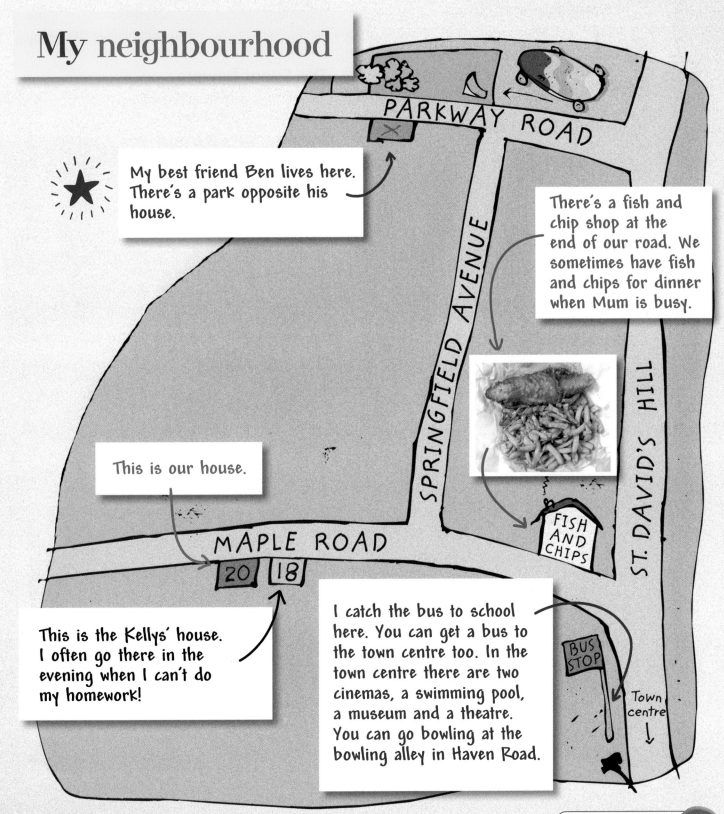

My best friend Ben lives here. There's a park opposite his house.

There's a fish and chip shop at the end of our road. We sometimes have fish and chips for dinner when Mum is busy.

This is our house.

This is the Kellys' house. I often go there in the evening when I can't do my homework!

I catch the bus to school here. You can get a bus to the town centre too. In the town centre there are two cinemas, a swimming pool, a museum and a theatre. You can go bowling at the bowling alley in Haven Road.

PARKWAY ROAD

SPRINGFIELD AVENUE

ST. DAVID'S HILL

FISH AND CHIPS

MAPLE ROAD

20 18

BUS STOP

Town centre

Module 5

Today and tomorrow

In Module 5 you study

Grammar

- Present continuous
- Object pronouns
- Present continuous used for the future
- Suggestions
- The future with *going to*

Vocabulary

- Names of clothes
- Football
- Future time expressions
- Weather vocabulary

so that you can

- Talk about things in progress at the moment
- Play a guessing game
- Describe what you're wearing now
- Say what you usually/never/ sometimes wear
- Talk about future arrangements
- Make and reply to suggestions
- write a message to a friend
- Describe plans and intentions
- Talk about the weather
- Write a holiday postcard

The Silent Powers
Chapter 7 – Pictures in the water
Chapter 8 – The meeting

Life and culture
Sports fans
An exchange visit

Coursework 5

My clothes
You describe the sort of clothes you like, and the things you usually wear.

What's it about?

What can you say about the pictures?

Now match the pictures with sentences 1–5.

1 Are you dreaming again?
2 She's wearing a red, white and black scarf.
3 Let's go bowling.
4 We're going to see the blue whale.
5 She's writing a postcard.

9 At the moment

STEP 1

In Step 1 you study
- present continuous

so that you can
- talk about things in progress at the moment

10 pm

12 am

1 Listening *And it's a goal!*

a 🔊 Close your book and listen. What's on TV?

b 🔊 Listen again and choose the right answer to the questions.

1 Who's playing?
   a France and Colombia.
   b Brazil and France.

2 How many people are watching the match?
   a A billion.   b A million.

3 What's the score?
   a Three–two. (3–2)   b Three all. (3–3)

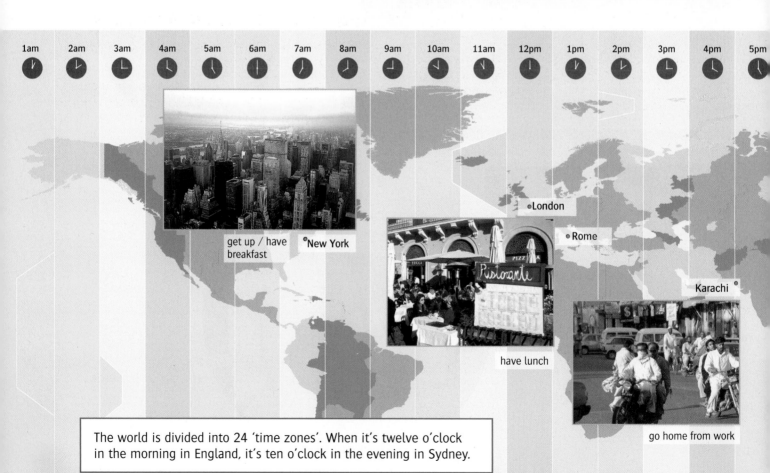

1am 2am 3am 4am 5am 6am 7am 8am 9am 10am 11am 12pm 1pm 2pm 3pm 4pm 5pm

get up / have breakfast
New York

London
Rome
Karachi

have lunch

go home from work

The world is divided into 24 'time zones'. When it's twelve o'clock in the morning in England, it's ten o'clock in the evening in Sydney.

2 Presentation
They're watching the match

a 🔊 **Close your book and listen. What's the score at the end of the conversation?**

The Kellys are watching the World Cup Final. The telephone's ringing. It's Annie in Australia!

MR KELLY: Hello.

ANNIE: Hi! It's Annie!

MR KELLY: Annie! How are you? What are you doing?

ANNIE: I'm watching the match, of course. What about you? Are you watching it?

MR KELLY: Yes, of course! I'm wearing my green and yellow scarf. Sue's sitting next to me. Joe and Sadie are arguing, as usual. Joe's supporting Brazil and Sadie's supporting France. Hang on a minute, Annie!

JOE: Brazil have got another goal!

b 🔊 **Listen again and follow in your book. Then answer the questions.**

1 What are the Kellys doing?
2 What's Mr Kelly wearing?
3 Where's Mrs Kelly sitting?
4 Why are Joe and Sadie arguing?

3 Key grammar
Present continuous: Wh- *questions; affirmative*

Complete the answers.

> What are you wearing? I _____ wearing a scarf.
> What's Sue doing? She _____ sitting next to Mr Kelly.
> What are Joe and Sadie doing? They _____ arguing.
>
> *We use the present continuous for things in progress at the moment.*

G ➤ 4a, c, d, 14

4 Practice

a **Make questions.**

1 *What's Annie doing?*

1 What / Annie doing ?
2 What / you doing ?
3 Where / Mr Kelly sitting ?
4 Where / you sitting ?
5 What / Joe and Sadie watching ?

b **Ask and answer the questions in 4a.**

(What's Annie doing?) (She's watching the match.)

5 Reading and speaking *The World Cup*

a **Read the text, then look at the map. Is everyone watching TV at the moment?**

The World Cup started in 1930. Now football is popular all over the world. It's the World Cup Final today and a billion people are watching the match! But what about the other 5.6 billion people in the world? What are they doing?

b **Ask and answer questions about the photos.**

(What are they doing in New York?)

(They're getting up.)

6 Writing *What's happening?*

Use what you know

What's happening at the moment? Write as many things as you can. Begin with the time, the day and the date.

It's half past ten on Tuesday, 28th April. I'm sitting in the classroom. My friend is ...

6pm 7pm 8pm 9pm 10pm 11pm 12am

Bangkok   have dinner

Canberra Sydney   Everyone's asleep.
Wellington

go to bed

Unit 9   95

In Step 2 you study
- present continuous: negative; questions and short answers
- object pronouns

so that you can
- talk about present actions
- play a guessing game

1 Presentation *Are you listening?*

a What can you say about the photo? What's happening?

b 🔲 Listen to Joe and his teacher and follow in your book. Then choose the right description.

a Joe's playing football.
b Joe's talking to his teacher.
c Joe's dreaming.

I've got the ball and I'm running towards the goal. The fans are shouting, 'Come on, Joe!' ... I'm not sitting in the classroom. Mrs Barker isn't saying 'Joe, you aren't listening!'. We aren't doing a chemistry test. I'm playing football in the World Cup!

Joe, you aren't listening!
Joe, are you dreaming again?

2 Key grammar *Present continuous: negative; questions and short answers*

Complete the table.

I	'm not	
Joe /He/She	_____	listening.
You/We/They	_____	

Am I		
_____ he/she	dreaming?	
_____ you/we/they		

Yes, I _____ .	No, I'm not.
Yes, he/she _____ .	No, he/she _____ .
Yes, you/we/they are.	No, you/we/they _____ .

Ⓖ➔ 4b-d

3 Practice

a Complete the sentences.

Joe ¹ *'s sitting* (sit) in the classroom. He and his friends ² _____ (do) a chemistry test. But Joe ³ _____ (not listen) to the teacher. Mrs Barker ⁴ _____ (say) 'You ⁵ _____ (not listen), Joe! ⁶ _____ you _____ (dream) again, Joe?'

b **Test a friend** Make at least one negative sentence. Your friend says if it is true or false.

I'm not eating an ice cream.   True!

4 Speaking

Think of an action and mime it. Can the class guess what you're doing?

A: Are you eating a pizza?
B: No, I'm not.
C: Are you eating a piece of melon?
B: Yes, I am. Your turn now!

Try this!
Write the right sentence:
jo ean dhisf rien dsar edo ingac hem is tryt est

c Match the questions with the answers, then ask and answer.

1 Are Joe and his friends at a football match?
2 Are they doing a chemistry test?
3 Is Joe listening to his teacher?
4 Is he dreaming?

a Yes, he is.
b No, he isn't.
c Yes, they are.
d No, they aren't.

5 Key pronunciation /ɪŋ/

🔊 Listen to the rhythm drill, then join in. Practise the -ing sound.

A: Help! It's chasing me.
B: Don't worry. You're dreaming.
A: Help! Help! I can't escape.
B: Don't worry. You're dreaming.
A: Help! Help! Help! Help!
   I'm falling. I'm falling.
B: You aren't falling. You're dreaming.
   Wake up. You're only dreaming.
A: Oh! What a horrible dream!

6 Presentation *Everybody loves me!*

a 🔊 Listen and follow in your book. Then put the pictures in the right order.

Joe's got the ball. And it's a goal! The fans are shouting 'We love **you**, Joe!' Joe's waving at **them** and he's smiling. Joe's mum is waving too, but he can't see **her**. She isn't at the match. She's watching **it** on TV. It's the end of the match now. A photographer is shouting 'Joe, look at **me**!' Two girls are saying 'Joe, come and talk to **us**.' Suddenly Joe is famous and everybody loves **him**.

b Use the sentences in the story to describe each picture.

7 Key grammar
Object pronouns

Complete the table with object pronouns.

I	➤	me
you	➤	....
he	➤	....
she	➤	....
it	➤	....
we	➤	....
they	➤	....

Ⓖ➤ 25

8 Practice

Complete the sentences.

1 I've got some new glasses.
   Do you like *them* ?
2 Sadie's singing in the bath.
   Can you hear .... ?
3 I'm trying to take a photo.
   Please look at .... !
4 Your room's in an awful mess.
   You must tidy .... !
5 I can't find my shoes. Can
   you see .... ?
6 Where's Ben? I can't find
   ....
7 You aren't listening! I'm
   talking to ....
8 We're going now. Are you
   coming with .... ?

9 Speaking
A guessing game

Use what you know

Make sentences with *it, him, her* or *them*. Your friends must guess what it is, or who it is.

A: I'm looking at them.
B: Your shoes!
A: I can see it in my bag.
B: Your pen!
A: You're sitting next to her.
B: Caterina!

In Step 3 you study
- names of clothes

so that you can
- describe what you're wearing now
- say what you usually/never/ sometimes wear

1 Key vocabulary *Clothes*

⏱ Look at the pictures. How many of these things can you see in the classroom? You've got three minutes!

1 a jacket

2 a coat

3 a raincoat

4 a sweater

5 a top

6 a skirt

7 a dress

8 jeans

9 trousers

10 shorts

11 socks

12 shoes

13 trainers

14 sandals

15 boots

16 glasses

17 sunglasses

18 gloves

19 a belt

20 a scarf

21 a hat

 Listen and say the words.

2 Listening *Outside the stadium*

a 📻 Listen to Jack and Ben. Who's got the tickets for the match?

It's Saturday afternoon. Exeter City are playing Bristol Rovers today. Jack and Ben are outside the football stadium. They're trying to find Lisa.

b 📻 Listen again and answer the questions.

1 What's Lisa wearing?
2 What's she carrying?
3 What's her hat like?
4 Does she wear it every day?
5 When does she wear it?

3 Writing and speaking

What about you? How many true sentences can you make using the verb *wear*? ⏱ You've got four minutes!

I never wear gloves. I sometimes wear shorts, but I'm not wearing shorts today.

4 Speaking *An observation test!*

Use what you know

Work with a friend. Sit 'back to back'. Describe what your partner is wearing.

A: You're wearing black trainers.
B: My trainers aren't black. They're blue.
A: You're wearing a belt. I think it's brown.
B: Yes, that's right.

CHAPTER 7

Pictures in the water

Everything is quiet on the bridge now, but Sophie is scared. She's looking at the river and she's thinking about her friends and her flat in London. She wants to go home.

Suddenly, she can see something in the water. Is she dreaming? No. The picture in the water is real.

She can see a hill and a cave. There's a face in the water too. It's the White Lady.

'Well done, Sophie! The Red Queen is trying to destroy the Silent Powers, but now she knows you're strong. Don't be scared. We're with you all the time. We must talk to you again. Come with Epona tomorrow …'

Now the picture is changing and Sophie can see the Red Queen.

'Work with me, Sophie. Give me the moonstone, then you can be free. You can go home and be happy again, in the ordinary world. Look at me, Sophie! Look at me!'

Before Sophie can look into the Red Queen's eyes, something is pulling her arm. It's Cabal. He's pulling her towards Hunter's Wood. He's taking her back to Seth's house.

- Find the meaning of ⌐, the sign in the river. Look at the seven pairs of words. The same letter is missing in each of the two words. Write the missing letters.

1 _ an   ca _ era
2 _ ou   e _ e
3 ea _ t   we _ t
4 ho _   _ own
5 hous _   p _ rson
6 _ adio   wate _
7 _ ellow   happ _

The missing letters make the word '_ _ _ _ _ _ _'.

Extra exercises

1 Choose the right word.

1 Can you see (*him* / *he*)?
2 Where's my mobile? Can you see (*it* / *her*)?
3 A big gorilla is looking at (*I* / *me.*)
4 I don't like vegetables. Do you like (*they* / *them*)?
5 Paul is coming to the beach with (*us* / *we*).
6 I can't find my scarf. Where is (*she* / *it*)?
7 Lisa doesn't know. Don't ask (*she* / *her*).

2 Choose the right words.

1 Ben and Lisa .... a football match on TV.
  a is watching
  b watching
  c are watching
2 Joe isn't .... to his teacher.
  a watching
  b listening
  c dreaming
3 Are you .... Brazil or France in this match?
  a seeing
  b supporting
  c going
4 A: What's Barney doing?
  B: He .... the piano.
  a 's playing
  b plays
  c play
5 Joe's playing football. He's .... his new trainers.
  a carrying
  b wearing
  c buying

3 Put the words in the right order and make questions.

1 doing / are / what / you ?
2 are / crisps / my / eating / you ?
3 sitting / where / Sadie / 's ?
4 Mr / wearing / what / 's / Kelly ?
5 going / 's / Joe / where ?
6 many / watching / how / are / people / match / the ?

4 Now match the answers with the questions in Exercise 3.

a No, I'm not.
b To school, I think.
c A billion.
d Next to Lisa.
e A green and yellow scarf.
f I'm listening to my new CD.

5 Complete the conversations.

1 Sadie's singing in the shower.
  a Yes, I can hear her.
  b That's enough.
  c Yes, it's in a mess.
2 What's the football score?
  a 2 billion.
  b Four all.
  c Three goals.
3 Joe's class are having a chemistry test.
  a How many?
  b What's the score?
  c Is it difficult?
4 What's Sadie's hat like?
  a No, she doesn't.
  b It's red.
  c Yes, she is.
5 Are you cooking the dinner today?
  a No, you aren't.
  b Chicken and vegetables.
  c Yes, I am.

6 Which word is the odd one out?

1 coat   hat   ice cream   raincoat   jacket
2 we   him   she   they   I
3 score   fan   rug   goal   ball
4 socks   shorts   gloves   stairs   trainers
5 talking   singing   dreaming   shouting   speaking

7 How do you say these sentences in your language?

1 Hang on a minute.
2 What's the score? – It's three all.
3 It's your turn now.
4 That's right.
5 The fans are shouting, 'Come on Joe!'
6 Football is popular all over the world.

Extra reading

Sports fans

What's your favourite sport?
Which sports are popular in the UK?

Football

'My favourite team is Manchester United and I go to all their matches with my son. The matches are usually on Saturday afternoon, or sometimes on Sunday. We often travel a long way to see them. My son has got autographs of his favourite players and one day he wants to be a Manchester United football player!'

Cricket

'Cricket's popular in the UK and it's also the national sport of Australia, India and Pakistan. Every year I take a week's holiday and go to watch England play an international match. The matches usually start at eleven o'clock and finish in the evening. They often continue for four or five days.'

Motor Racing

'Our favourite sport is motor racing. We usually go to the British Grand Prix at Silverstone in July to watch the Ferrari team. We always arrive early and we take a picnic lunch. For us, it's the best day of the year.'

Tennis

'The Wimbledon tennis championship takes place in June. It's famous all over the world. Half a million people go every year. It's often difficult to buy tickets for the final. People queue for a long time – sometimes all night. This year I'm at the front of the queue – with my sleeping bag and lots of food!'

ABOUT WIMBLEDON

People at the Wimbledon tennis championship eat 27,000 kilograms of English strawberries in a fortnight!

Task

Are these sentences true or false?

1 Football matches are usually on Saturday morning.
2 The different football clubs play all over the country.
3 Cricket is popular in India.
4 International cricket matches are often quite long.
5 The Wimbledon tennis championship takes place in the winter.
6 It isn't easy to buy tickets for the Wimbledon final.
7 The Grand Prix is a horse race.
8 Silverstone is the name of a racing car.

10 Plans

STEP 1

In Step 1 you study
- future time expressions
- present continuous used for the future
- suggestions

so that you can
- talk about future arrangements
- make and reply to a suggestion

1 Key vocabulary *Time expressions*

a Copy the time line. Put the time expressions in the right place.

today tomorrow at the moment next month next week
next year at the weekend now tonight this evening

Present   Future
1 today 2 _____ 3 _____ 4 _____ 5 _____ 6 _____ 7 _____ 8 _____ 9 _____ 10 next year

[🔊] Listen and check.

b Complete the sentences.

1 Tomorrow is _____ (the name of the day).
2 Next month is _____ (the name of the month).
3 The date next Monday is _____ .
4 _____ means 'on Saturday and Sunday'.
5 _____ I'm doing sentence number five.

2 Presentation
Making arrangements

a Read the emails. Match the three invitations with the three replies.

Number one goes with number five.

[🔊] Listen and check.

b Look at the emails and answer the questions.

1 What's Anna doing on Saturday?
2 Is Danny going to Anna's party?
3 Is Tom going home after school?
4 Is Kim busy at nine o'clock tomorrow?
5 What time is Kim meeting Lucia?
6 Where are Kim and Lucia meeting?

---

1 Hi ???,
I'm having a party on Saturday.
Can you come?
Anna

2 Hi ???,
Sorry, but I can't. I'm going to the dentist after school. Let's play at the weekend. Is that OK?
Tom

3 Hi ???,
Are you busy after school? Shall we play football?
Rick.

4 Dear ???,
Yes, that's fine. I'm having a guitar lesson at 9 o'clock. Why don't we meet outside the sports centre at 10.30?
Kim

5 Dear ???,
Yes, I can. Thanks very much. See you on Saturday. Danny
PS Is Lucia coming?

6 Hi ???,
Shall we go swimming tomorrow morning? Are you free?
Lucia

3 Key grammar
Present continuous used for the future

Which column (A, B or C) shows that the sentences are about the future?

A	B	C
I'm		this evening.
She's	having a party	tomorrow.
They're		next Friday.

 G 4f

4 Practice

a Complete the sentences about the future with these verbs.

have   go   watch   meet   come

1 *Lucia's coming to my house after school.*

1 Lucia / to my house after school
2 We / Danny at seven o'clock
3 I / to the dentist tomorrow
4 We / an English test on Friday
5 Tom / a video with Rick this evening

b Test a friend Make two sentences with the present continuous, one about the present and one about the future. Your friend says 'present' or 'future'.

A: I'm wearing a black T-shirt today.
B: Present.
A: I'm playing basketball next Saturday.
B: Future.

5 Speaking

a Work with a friend and practise the conversation.

A: What are you doing <u>this evening</u>?
B: I'm <u>meeting some friends</u>. What about you?
A: I'm <u>staying at home</u>.

b Change the <u>underlined</u> words in 5a and make another conversation. Here are some ideas:

go to the beach   play volleyball
visit my grandparents   go shopping

> **Try this!**
> What do these abbreviations mean?
> Sat. Dec. Mon. Sun. Feb.
> Oct. Wed. Fri. Jan. Tues.
> Sept. Thurs. Nov.

6 Key grammar   *Suggestions*

How do you say these sentences in your language?

> **Let's** play at the weekend.
> **Shall we** go swimming?
> **Why don't we** meet outside the sports centre?

G 26

7 Practice

Complete the conversation with these sentences.

Shall we watch TV?   Let's stay at home.
Let's look.   Why don't we go bowling?

A: I'm bored.
B: ¹ ....
A: No, I'm tired.
   ² ....
B: OK. ³ ....
A: Is it *Friends* this evening?
B: I'm not sure.
   ⁴ ....

8 Speaking

Work with a friend. Say a sentence from A. Can your friend make a suggestion from B?

(I'm bored.)   (Shall we go to the cinema?)

A		B	
1	I'm tired.	a	Shall we go to the cinema?
2	I'm bored.	b	Let's have a sandwich.
3	I'm hot.	c	Why don't we go home?
4	I'm hungry.	d	Shall we buy a drink?
5	I'm thirsty.	e	Let's open the windows.

9 Writing   *Messages*

Use what you know

Work with a friend. Write a message with a suggestion. Use the time expressions in Exercise 1. Then read your friend's message and write a reply.

> *Dear Renaldo*
> *What are you doing this evening?*
> *Shall we go swimming?*
> *Karl*

In Step 2 you study
- the future with *going to*

so that you can
- talk about plans and intentions
- make a notice of 'good intentions'

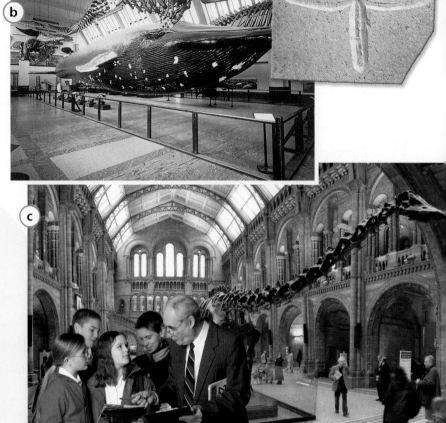

1 Presentation

What are you going to do?

a Look at the photos (a–c) of the Natural History Museum in London. Find a dinosaur, a whale and a fossil.

b 🔊 Close your book and listen. Is it the beginning or the end of Jack's visit ?

Jack's class are visiting the Natural History Museum with their teacher, Mr White. They're in the entrance hall and they're looking at their brochures.

MR WHITE: Jack, what are you going to do?

JACK: I'm going to draw that dinosaur.

MR WHITE: That's a good idea. And what about you, Ben?

BEN: I'm going to look at the fossils. Gallery 31, 'Fossils from Britain'.

LISA: Mr White's an old fossil.

SADIE: Be quiet, Lisa! He can hear you.

MR WHITE: And Sadie and Lisa, what are you going to do?

LISA: We're going to see the blue whale in Gallery 23.

SADIE: Lisa's going to take some photos.

MR WHITE: That's nice. Well, I'm going to visit Gallery 11. Listen, everyone! Let's meet here at one o'clock. OK?

CLASS: Yes, Mr White.

LISA: Gallery 11. What's he going to look at, Sadie?

SADIE: Let's see. Gallery 11. Here it is. Oh! It's the Waterhouse Café.

c 🔊 Listen again and follow in your book. Then answer the questions.

1. Who's going to take some photos?
2. Who's going to draw a dinosaur?
3. Who's going to have a drink?
4. Who's going to see the blue whale?
5. Who's going to look at the fossils?

2 Key grammar going to

Complete the table.

I'm He's/She's We're/You're/They're	going _____	take a photo.
I'm not He/She isn't We/You/They aren't		look at the whale.
Are you _____ he/she _____ they	going to	have a drink?
Yes, I am/he is/they _____ . No, I _____ / he _____ / they aren't.		

We use going to *+ verb to talk about plans and intentions.*

Ⓖ▶ 8

3 Practice

a Put the words in the right order and make sentences.

1 going / take / we're / photos / to / some
2 to / fossil / going / draw / he / a / isn't
3 at / look / to / the/ going / they're / dinosaurs
4 whale / going / you / blue / the / see / to / are ?
5 of / to / a / tea / I'm / have / going / cup

b **Role play** If you have time, imagine you're at the museum and act a short conversation. Use words from 1b.

4 Reading and speaking
A dinosaur, please.

a Read the prices of things at the museum. Find two things that you want to buy.

Café

Apple juice, orange juice	£1.50
Mineral water	£1.60
Tea	£1.25
Coffee	£1.25
Pizza	£4.95
Sandwiches:	
• Cheese and tomato	£3.25
• Ham	£3.30
• Chicken and salad	£3.45
Mixed Salad	£2.95
Yoghurt	£1.40
Fruit	95p

Shop

Postcards	80p
Posters	£8
Pens	£1.60
T-shirts	£9.95
Dinosaurs	£4.70
Whales	£4.30

b You've got £10. How are you going to spend your money? Tell the class.

> I'm going to have a ham sandwich and some orange juice. I'm going to buy a plastic dinosaur.

5 Listening
Song

🔊 Close your book and listen. Make four sentences from the song. Use *going to* and the words in the lists.

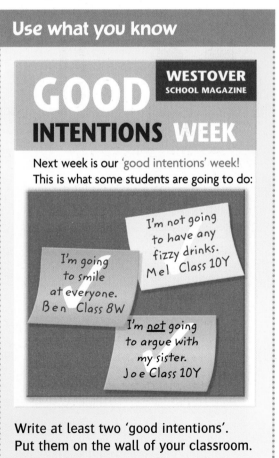

I'm going to ...

catch   find   leave   be

free   this job   a better place   a train

6 Key pronunciation /ə/

🔊 Listen and repeat the sentences. Practise the stress and the 'weak form' of *to* /tə/.

1 I'm going to **catch** a **train**.
2 I'm going to **leave** this **job**.
3 I'm going to **be** **free**.

7 Writing *My resolutions*

Use what you know

WESTOVER SCHOOL MAGAZINE

GOOD INTENTIONS WEEK

Next week is our 'good intentions' week! This is what some students are going to do:

> I'm going to smile at everyone. Ben Class 8W ✓

> I'm not going to have any fizzy drinks. Mel Class 10Y

> I'm **not** going to argue with my sister. Joe Class 10Y ✓

Write at least two 'good intentions'. Put them on the wall of your classroom.

In Step 3 you study
● weather vocabulary
so that you can
● talk about the weather
● write a holiday postcard

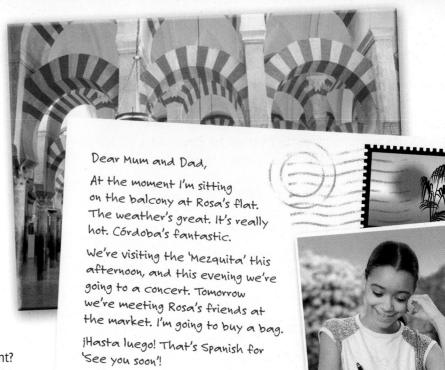

1 Reading
A postcard from Mel

It's half term and Mel is staying with her Spanish pen friend, Rosa.

a Read the postcard. Where is Mel?

b ⏱ Answer the questions. You've got two minutes!

1 What's Mel doing at the moment?
2 What's she doing this afternoon?
3 Are Mel and Rosa busy tomorrow?
4 What's Mel going to buy?

Dear Mum and Dad,

At the moment I'm sitting on the balcony at Rosa's flat. The weather's great. It's really hot. Córdoba's fantastic.

We're visiting the 'Mezquita' this afternoon, and this evening we're going to a concert. Tomorrow we're meeting Rosa's friends at the market. I'm going to buy a bag.

¡Hasta luego! That's Spanish for 'See you soon'!

Love,

Mel.

2 Key vocabulary *The weather*

🔊 Listen and say the sentences. Then ask and answer.

> What's the weather like today?

1 It's hot.

2 It's cold.

3 It's cloudy.

4 It's windy.

5 It's sunny.

6 It's foggy.

7 It's raining.

8 It's snowing.

3 Writing *A holiday postcard*

Use what you know

Imagine you're on holiday. Think of an interesting place and write a postcard. Answer these questions.

What are you doing at the moment? What's the weather like? What are you doing this evening / tomorrow?

CHAPTER 8

The meeting

The next morning Sophie is talking to Seth at breakfast.

'Seth, I want to go riding this morning. Is that OK?'

'But it's windy and it's raining. Why don't you go this afternoon? '

'I can't. A friend's phoning me from New York this afternoon.'

Outside in the garden Sophie can see Cabal.

— ● ● ● —

Soon Sophie and Epona are following Cabal through Hunter's Wood.

Mr Neil and the White Lady are waiting for them at the Circle of Seven. Sophie wants to ask a lot of questions.

'Mr Neil, what's happening? I'm scared.'

'Don't worry, Sophie. This morning you must go to King's Hill and open the Gate of Rings.'

'What's the Gate of Rings?'

'It's your last test, Sophie.'

'Are you and the White Lady going to come with me?'

'No, we aren't. You must find the hill. Do you remember the text message?'

'Yes, I've got it in my pocket.'

'That text message is a map.'

Sophie is watching Epona. The horse is nervous.

'Mr Neil, what's the matter with Epona?'

'The king is calling her. You must leave now. Good luck, Sophie! '

● Find the meaning of **M**, the sign in the middle of the Circle of Seven.

Use this code and find the missing word.

ABCDEFGHIJKLMNOPQRSTUVWXYZ

If 8 18 20 13 means *SIGN*, what does 7 22 26 14 mean?

Sophie isn't alone. Mr Neil and the White Lady are helping her. She and her friends are a ' __ __ __ __ '.

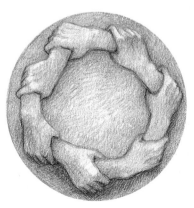

Extra exercises

1 Choose the right word.

1 I'm going to the dentist _____ Saturday.
  a in
  b on
  c at

2 I'm tired. _____ we stop for a minute?
  a Let's
  b Shall
  c Why

3 The weather's great! It's really _____ .
  a cloudy
  b windy
  c sunny

4 It's my birthday next _____ .
  a day
  b afternoon
  c week

5 Are we near the station? _____ we look at the map?
  a Shall
  b Do
  c Don't

2 Read the text and choose the right word for each space.

> Dear Kelly,
> I'm on holiday [1]_____ Paris. It's a fantastic city!
> The weather [2]_____ very good. It's cold and
> [3]_____ raining. [4]_____ evening I'm going to Notre
> Dame and [5]_____ morning I'm visiting the Eiffel
> Tower with my friend, Marie.
> Love,
> Max

1	a in	b on	c at
2	a aren't	b is	c isn't
3	a it	b it's	c there's
4	a That	b The	c This
5	a next	b tomorrow	c yesterday

3 Do these sentences refer to the present or the future? Write *Present* or *Future*.

1 Sadie is visiting her grandmother next week.
2 Look! It's snowing.
3 Kelly's wearing her favourite jeans today.
4 I'm going into town tomorrow.
5 I'm playing volleyball after school.
6 What's Karen doing now?

4 Gill is asking Tom about his school trip next week. Complete the conversation.

GILL: [1]_____ next week?
TOM: To the Natural History Museum, in London.
GILL: [2]_____ by train?
TOM: No, we're going by bus.
GILL: [3]_____ there?
TOM: We're going to see the Blue Whale Exhibition.
GILL: [4]_____ the dinosaurs too?
TOM: Yes, and the 'Fossils from Britain'.
GILL: Have you got any money to spend?
TOM: Yes, I've got £10. I'm [5]_____ a poster.

5 Complete the conversations.

1 What's the weather like?
  a Yes, it's great.
  b Yes, I'm hot.
  c It's foggy.

2 When are you going to the dentist?
  a At the moment.
  b Yesterday.
  c Next month.

3 I'm thirsty.
  a Why don't we go to the cinema?
  b Let's have a drink.
  c Shall we go for a walk?

4 Are you busy after school?
  a Yes, that's fine.
  b No, I'm not.
  c Sorry, I can't.

5 Can you come to my party on Sunday?
  a Are you free?
  b No, sorry. I'm busy.
  c Let's have a party.

6 How do you say these sentences in your language?

1 Shall we have a drink?
2 Let's meet at one o'clock.
3 What's the weather like?
4 That's a good idea.
5 We're going to Australia. – That's nice.
6 Can you see my mobile? – Yes, here it is.

Extra reading

An exchange visit

Have you got any friends in other countries? Which countries do you want to visit?

Donna Mills is from Castleton High School in Glasgow, Scotland. At the moment, she's at school in the USA. She's on a six-month school exchange visit at Hotchkiss Junior High School in Kansas.

'I'm very happy here in Hotchkiss. Some of my classes are easy and others are quite hard but all my teachers are fantastic. I'm in the choir and next Saturday we're singing in front of the whole school. I'm also in the basketball team and we're playing in Oklahoma next month. After school I sometimes go to the International Club, a special club for exchange students. There are students from all over the world — Japan, Africa, Sweden, Venezuela. We usually meet on Wednesday afternoon and we talk about our life here. It's really interesting. Hotchkiss is a great school, everybody is friendly and helpful.

My host family is also very kind. They live on a big ranch and they've got lots of animals. When the weather's hot and sunny we go horse riding or we look after the cows — it's great fun. Next week is half term, no school for a week, and my family is taking me to New York. We're going to visit the Empire State Building and lots of other places. I'm really excited!'

ABOUT EXCHANGE VISITS

Students in the UK go on exchange visits to other countries in Europe, to the USA, Asia, New Zealand and South America. And a lot of British schools visit schools in other countries on the Internet.

Task

Answer the questions.

1 Where's Donna's home?
2 What sport does she play at Hotchkiss?
3 When does the International Club meet?
4 What do the students do at the club?
5 Where's Donna staying?
6 When's she going to New York?
7 What's she going to do there?

Language summary

1 Present continuous

We use the present continuous tense to describe things that are 'in progress' now.

You're having an English lesson.
Look! It's raining.

Affirmative			Negative		
I'm You're He's She's It's We're You're They're	coming. leaving.		I'm not You aren't He isn't She isn't It isn't We aren't You aren't They aren't	going. shouting.	

I'm = I am   You're = You are   He's = He is aren't = are not   isn't = is not

Questions

Am I			Yes, I am.	No, I'm not.
Are you/we/they	dreaming? waiting?		Yes, you/we/ they are.	No, you/we/ they aren't.
Is he/she/it			Yes, he/she / it is.	No, he/she/ it isn't.

What	is he/she/it are you/we/they	doing?

Check that you can

1.1 • describe things 'in progress'.

Make true sentences using these verbs.

wear   have   do   use   sit   rain

1 *I'm not wearing a white T-shirt today.*

1 I / a white T-shirt today
2 Our teacher / a computer at the moment
3 I / near the window today
4 We / our lunch at the moment
5 It / at the moment
6 I / an English exercise

1.2 • make questions for these answers.

1 *Where are you going?*
1 To the supermarket.
2 A letter to my gran.
3 To the bowling alley.
4 An article about dolphins.
5 A programme about sky surfing.

2 Present continuous + future time expressions

We can use the present continuous tense to talk about arrangements for the future.

I'm meeting Superman Lucia's having a party We're going to New York	at five o'clock. this evening. tonight. tomorrow. at the weekend. next week. on Saturday. in July.

Check that you can

• use future time expressions.

Complete the sentences with *at, in* or *on*.

1 Jack's going to Manchester __at__ the weekend.
2 Monsoon are playing at our school _____ Friday.
3 I'm going home _____ four o'clock.
4 Sadie's cousins are coming to England _____ August.
5 Mel's going swimming _____ the weekend.
6 We're having a maths test _____ Monday.

Now make a question and answer for each sentence.

1 *When's Jack going to Manchester?*
  At the weekend.

3 The future with *going to*

We use *going to* + verb to describe future plans and intentions:

I'm going to write to the president.
Jack's going to cook the dinner.

Affirmative

I'm You're He's/She's We're You're They're	going to	have a drink. buy some postcards.

Negative

I'm not You/We/ They aren't He/She isn't	going to	visit the museum. take any photos.

Questions

Are you/we/they Is he/she	going to	dance? get up?

Yes, I am.   No, I'm not. Yes, he/she is.   No, he/she isn't. Yes, you/we/they are. No, you/we/they aren't.

What	is he are they	going to do?

Check that you can

- talk about plans and intentions.

What are these people going to do? Guess!

1 She's going to have an omelette for dinner.

1 Lucia's buying some eggs.
2 Rick's going into the living room.
3 Danny's on the train.
4 Tom's making a shopping list.
5 Kim's got a pencil in her hand.

Now ask and answer questions about their plans.

> What's Lucia going to do?

4 Object pronouns

Object pronouns always go after the verb:
*Where's my anorak? Have you got **it**?*
*Where are my trainers? I can't find **them**.*

A large gorilla is looking at	me/you/him/her/ it/us/you/them.

Check that you can

- use object pronouns.

Complete the sentences with *me, you, him* etc.

1 I can't find <u>Lisa</u>. Can you see <u>*her*</u> ?
2 We can't find <u>Ben</u>. Can you see _____ ?
3 I need my <u>dictionary</u>. Where is _____ ?
4 <u>We're</u> in a hurry. Can you help _____ , please?

5 Don't stand in front of _____ . <u>I</u> can't see.
6 You can have <u>my chips</u>. I don't want _____ .
7 <u>Sadie's</u> talking. Don't interrupt _____ .
8 <u>You</u> like me and I like _____ .

5 Making suggestions

We can use these three expressions to make suggestions:

Let's	go to the Natural History Museum.
Shall we Why don't we	go to the Natural History Museum?

Check that you can

- make and respond to suggestions.

Think of a suggestion for each response.

1 Shall we go to the skate park?

1 Not now. I'm busy.
2 I'm not thirsty, thanks.
3 Sorry, but I'm busy tomorrow.
4 I can't. I'm doing my homework.
5 Not now. It's too hot!
6 I can't. I haven't got any money.

6 Present continuous or present simple?

We use the present continuous for things that are happening at the moment:
Don't interrupt. I'm talking, and you aren't listening.

We use the present simple for habits and things that are generally true:
I like gorillas. Bears eat fish.

Check that you can

- use the two present tenses in English.

Put the verbs in the correct form.

1 We often _____ (*go*) to a football match on Saturday.
2 Lisa's on the bus. She _____ (*go*) home.
3 I can't come now. I _____ (*eat*) my lunch.
4 You must wear a coat. It _____ (*snow*).
5 Jack usually _____ (*get up*) at 7.15.
6 Ben _____ (*not like*) history.

Vocabulary

Verbs

to buy
to carry
to dream
to drink
to eat
to go to school/work
to have a lesson /
   a party / a test
to meet
to ring
to run
to say
to shout
to sit
to smile
to spend (money)
to take (a photo)
to wave
to wear

Football

ball
fan
final
football stadium
goal
match
photographer
score
(to) support
team

Clothes

anorak
belt
boots
coat
dress
gloves
hat
jacket
jeans
raincoat
sandals
scarf
shoes
shorts
skirt
socks
sunglasses
sweater
T-shirt
top
trainers
trousers

The weather

It's cloudy.
It's cold.
It's foggy.
It's hot.
It's raining.
It's snowing.
It's sunny.
It's windy.

Making arrangements

Are you busy?
Are you free?
Is that OK?
See you on Saturday.
That's fine.

Expressions

At the moment.
Hang on a minute!
Here it is.
See you soon.
That's a good idea.
That's nice.
What's happening?
What's the weather like?

Study skills 5 Parts of speech

Possessive
adjective   noun   verb

My   teacher   thinks   I   am   brilliant!

pronoun   verb   adjective

Make a card game: 'Snap'! You need 24 white cards. Make:

8 'adjective' cards: | big | quiet | cold |

8 'noun' cards: | trousers | bike |

8 'verb' cards: | sing | run | buy |

Put the cards on the desk and find pairs of cards with the same part of speech.

How's it going?

● Your rating

Look again at pages 110–111. For each section give yourself a star rating:

Good ☆ ☆ ☆ Not bad ☆ ☆ I can't remember much ☆

● Vocabulary

Choose two titles in the Vocabulary list, then close your book. How many words can you remember for each topic?

● Test a friend

Look again at Units 9 and 10. Think of at least two questions, then ask a friend.

> How do you say ... in English?
> What can you see at the Natural History Museum?

● Write to your teacher

Write a short letter to your teacher in your own language. Say how things are going. Have you got any problems?

● Your Workbook

Complete the Learning diaries for Units 9 and 10.

Coursework 5 – All about me!

Read about Jack. Then describe your clothes. What sort of clothes do you like?
What do you usually wear? Use drawings, pictures and photos too.

My clothes

In this photo, I'm wearing my school uniform – black trousers, a white shirt, a blue jacket, a black top and black shoes.

I hate our uniform!

At the weekend, I usually wear jeans and trainers. My trainers are quite old but they're really comfortable. I don't like expensive clothes.

It rains a lot where I live, so I often wear an anorak to school.

We often buy our clothes at St. George's market.

This is my favourite T-shirt. It's got a picture of a car on it.

Module 6

Looking back

In Module 6 you study

Grammar

- Past simple of *be*
- Past simple: regular and irregular verbs

Vocabulary

- Names of occupations
- Past time expressions

so that you can

- Talk about people from the past
- Play a quiz game about famous people
- Write about an imaginary person's life
- Describe your early childhood
- Describe things that happened / didn't happen in the past
- Write a letter about an event in the past
- Write a diary
- Talk about your school year

The Silent Powers

Chapter 9 – King's Hill and the Gate of Rings
Chapter 10 – A horse for the king's men

Life and culture

From North to South
Quiz: The UK and the USA

Coursework 6

My life line
You write about important events in your life.

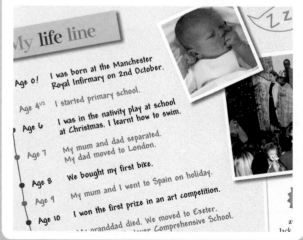

My life line

Age 0!   I was born at the Manchester Royal Infirmary on 2nd October.

Age 4½   I started primary school.

Age 6   I was in the nativity play at school at Christmas. I learnt how to swim.

Age 7   My mum and dad separated. My dad moved to London.

Age 8   We bought my first bike.

Age 9   My mum and I went to Spain on holiday.

Age 10   I won the first prize in an art competition.

What's it about?

What can you say about the pictures?

Now match the pictures with sentences 1–5.

1 He was a brilliant scientist.
2 She studied chimpanzees.
3 What did you like at primary school?
4 We didn't get their autographs.
5 They went to America.

In Step 1 you study
- names of occupations
- past simple of *be*

so that you can
- talk about people from the past
- play a quiz game about famous people

Fact or fiction?

① Pablo Picasso was a painter. He was Italian.

② William Shakespeare was an English writer. One of his plays was *Romeo and Juliet*.

③ Albert Einstein was an actor. He was born in Germany.

④ Maria Montessori was a famous teacher.

⑤ Kurt Cobain was a singer and guitarist.

⑥ The Beatles were British pop stars. There were four people in the group – John, Paul, George and Ringo.

⑦ Marie Skłodowska-Curie and Pierre Curie were scientists. They were born in France.

⑧ Christopher Columbus was an explorer. He was born in Italy.

⑨ George Washington and Abraham Lincoln were American film stars.

⑩ Sputnik 2 was a Russian spaceship. There was a dog called Laika on the spaceship. She was the first animal in space.

1 Key vocabulary
Occupations

Complete the sentences with these words.

writer   actor   actress   scientist
pop star   painter   singer   explorer

1 I'm a *pop star* .   2 We're *scientists* .

3 She's an _____ .   4 He's an _____ .

5 They're _____ .   6 We're _____ .

7 She's a _____ .   8 He's a _____ .

🔊 Listen and check.

2 Presentation   *Who were they?*

a ⏱ Work with a friend. Match the photos with the names in the quiz. You've got three minutes!

b 🔊 There are four mistakes in the quiz. Can you find them? Listen to the quiz and check.

c 🔊 Listen and read the sentences. Who is speaking?

1 Albert Einstein

1 I wasn't an actor. I was a scientist.
2 I wasn't born in France. I was born in Poland.
3 I wasn't Italian. I was Spanish.
4 We weren't film stars. We were presidents.

4 Practice

a Complete the questions with *was* or *were*.

1 .... Picasso a painter?
2 Who .... the Beatles?
3 .... they from Liverpool?
4 Who .... Christopher Columbus?
5 .... he American?
6 .... Laika the first animal in space?

b Ask and answer the questions in 4a.

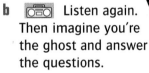

Was Picasso a painter?   Yes, he was.

c If you have time, ask and answer more questions about the people in the quiz.

5 Listening *Ghosts*

It's the middle of the night in an old house in the centre of Paris ...

a 🔊 Listen to the conversation. Can you guess the ghost's name?

b 🔊 Listen again. Then imagine you're the ghost and answer the questions.

1 *No, I wasn't.*

1 Were you born in Paris?
2 What nationality were you?
3 Were you happy at school?
4 Were you good at art?
5 Were you a teacher?
6 What was your name?

c Work with a friend and ask and answer the questions in 5b.

3 Key grammar was/were

Complete the table.

	was	
I/He/She/It	....	British.
You/We/They	....	American.
	weren't	
Was	he/she it	famous?
Were	you/they	

Yes, he .... / No, he wasn't.
Yes, they were. / No, they ....

G ▶ 3

6 Writing and speaking *Quiz*

Use what you know

Write at least two true or false sentences about people from the past and test your friends.

A: Salvador Dali was a painter.
B: True.
A: Paul Cezanne was a singer.
C: False! He was a painter.

In Step 2 you study
- past simple (affirmative): regular verbs

so that you can
- say what happened in the past
- write about an imaginary person's life

1

Jane Goodall is a zoologist.

1 Reading *Z is for zoo*

a Read the dictionary definitions, then complete this sentence:

The word *zoo* comes from the Greek word *zoion*. It means:

a to study   b place   c animal

> **zoo** (*plural* **zoos**) /zuː/ *noun*
> a place where animals are
> kept so that people can go
> and look at them
> **zoology** /zuːˈɒlədʒi/ *noun*
> the scientific study of animals
> **zoologist** /zuːˈɒlədʒɪst/
> *noun* a person who studies
> animals

b Are these sentences true or false? What do you think?

1 Zoologists work with animals.
2 They study animals' habits.
3 They always work in an office.
4 They sometimes travel to different countries.
5 They sometimes live in forests and jungles.
6 They want to learn more about animals' habits.

2 Presentation
She worked in Africa

a What can you say about the photos?

b 🔊 Listen to the text and follow in your book. Find a caption for photos 2, 3 and 4.

Jane Goodall was born in London. When she was a child, she loved animals. Her favourite books were about animals. When she was a teenager, she wanted to study wild animals in Africa. Her ambition never changed.

She finished school, and her first job was with a film company. But she worked in a hotel too, and she saved all her money. Then she travelled to Africa.

2

Jane studied chimpanzees. At first, they were scared of her, so she watched them from a distance. She used binoculars. But after three or four months, the animals accepted her. Then she lived in the forest and she watched the chimpanzees every day.

Now Jane is famous. She travels all over the world. She writes and teaches. You can read about her work on the Internet.

3

4

c Read the sentences about Jane's life. Put them in the right order. 1 b, 2 ...

a She arrived in Africa.

b When she was a child, she was interested in animals.

c Now she's famous and she goes all over the world.

d She studied the chimpanzees in the forest.

e She worked in a hotel too.

f She wanted to be a zoologist.

g She worked for a film company.

h She saved her money for a ticket to Africa.

3 Key grammar *Past simple: regular verbs*

a Complete the explanation.

I/You/He/She/We/You/They	worked in a hotel. wanted to be a zoologist.

work ➔ worked   want ➔ wanted

Regular verbs in the past simple end in _____ .

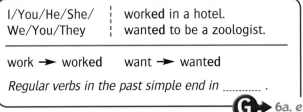 **6a, e**

b Look at the text again. Find more verbs in the past simple. Then copy and complete the table.

Present	Past
work	worked
live	1 _____
2 _____	studied
love	3 _____
travel	4 _____
want	5 _____

See Spelling notes, page 142.

4 Practice

a Complete the sentences with verbs in the past simple from 3b.

1 When I was three, I _wanted_ to be an actor.

2 When he was a teenager, my father _____ the Beatles.

3 Picasso _____ in France.

4 Laika _____ in a Russian spaceship.

5 Maria Montessori _____ at a school in Italy.

6 Albert Einstein _____ music at school.

b **Test a friend** Make at least one false sentence about Jane Goodall. Can your friend correct it?

> She wanted to study chemistry.

> No! She wanted to study wild animals.

5 Key pronunciation /d/ /t/ /ɪd/

a 📻 Listen to the rhythm drill, then join in.

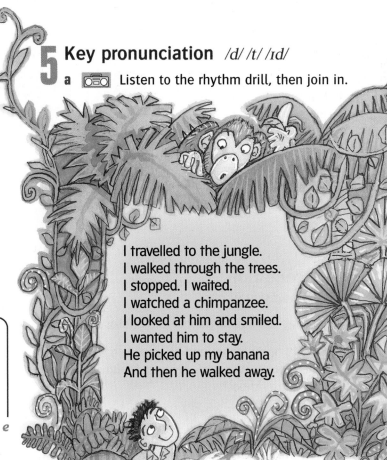

I travelled to the jungle.
I walked through the trees.
I stopped. I waited.
I watched a chimpanzee.
I looked at him and smiled.
I wanted him to stay.
He picked up my banana
And then he walked away.

b Match these verbs with their stress patterns.

wanted   looked   stopped   accepted   walked

1 ● picked   *looked*

2 ●● waited

6 Writing *A famous zoologist*

Use what you know

Write about an imaginary zoologist. Use words from the text in 2b but change some of the details, for example:

sharks – Australia   elephants – Africa
tigers – India   penguins – Antarctica

Follow this plan:

Paragraph 1: Enrico Lado was born ... .
When he was a child, he ... . He wanted ...
Paragraph 2: He travelled ... . He ...
Paragraph 3: Now he is famous. He ...

> **Try this!**
> Find the names of six jobs.
> RATCEHE CRODOT RUNSE
> TRACO CITISTENS LOZOTIGSO

STEP 3

In Step 3 you study
● past simple: *Wh-* questions
so that you can
● describe your early childhood

1 Presentation
What did you like?

a What can you say about the photos?

b 🔊 Listen and read about Ben's early childhood. Was Jack his best friend at primary school?

BEN: I was four when I started school. I was really nervous at first. I was scared of our teacher, because she shouted at us! I liked the books in the school library, and I liked Sports Day. But I hated maths.

My best friend was a boy called Darren. Jack's my best friend now, but he lived in Manchester when he was little.

When I was at primary school, I loved aeroplanes. I wanted to be a pilot. But I'm not so sure now.

c Imagine you're Ben. Answer the questions.

1 *When I was four.*
1 When did you start school, Ben?
2 Were you happy at first?
3 What did you like?
4 And what did you hate?
5 When you were little, what did you want to be?

d Now ask and answer the questions.

2 Key grammar   *Past simple:* Wh- *questions*

Complete the explanation.

What		you	like?
Who	did	Jack	live?
Where		he/she	
When		they	start school?

We make Wh- *questions in the past with a question word + _____ + subject + verb.*

G ➤ 6c, f, 14

3 Practice

a Read the sentences about Lisa's early childhood. Make a question for each sentence.

1 *Where did she play?*
1 Lisa played <u>in the park</u>.
2 She watched <u>a lot of cartoons</u> on TV.
3 School started <u>at nine o'clock</u>.
4 She arrived <u>at ten to nine</u>.
5 Her lessons finished <u>at twenty past three</u>.
6 She visited <u>her grandparents</u>.
7 She wanted to be <u>a teacher</u>.

b Ask and answer.

Where did she play?   She played in the park.

Remember!

Where **was** Ben's primary school?
We don't use did *with the verb* be (was/were).

4 Writing and speaking
Your early childhood

Use what you know

Write sentences about your childhood memories. Then interview a friend. Ask at least three questions.

What did you like at school?

CHAPTER 9

King's Hill and the Gate of Rings

Sophie and Epona followed a path through the wood. The horse stopped at the foot of a hill. Sophie looked at the first two lines of the text message. This was King's Hill. She was sure.

Suddenly, someone called her name. She turned round. Behind her there was a man in a long cloak, with a sword in his hand.

'Mr Neil? Is it you?'

'Yes, Sophie. But Mr Neil is Merlin too. I am Merlin, the wizard. Now we must open the Gate of Rings.'

Merlin touched the ground with his sword. There was an explosion and a gate appeared in the side of the hill.

'Open the gate, Sophie! Only you know the secret word.'

Sophie closed her eyes. There was a word in her head, but it wasn't clear. She heard a voice: 'You can never open the gate!' A strong red light filled her head. Then she touched the moonstone in her pocket. The red light disappeared and the word was clear. Sophie shouted. The gate opened and she looked into a dark cave.

She followed Merlin and Epona inside. The White Lady was there, with the Book of Signs. Sophie's name was on the open page.

- Look at King's Hill in the picture. What do the first two lines of the text message mean?
- Look at the gate and the third line of the text message. What do the five Rs mean?
- Look at the names 'Mr Neil' and 'Merlin'. Why are they similar?
- Find the meaning of ⚡, the sign in the picture. It's the secret word that Sophie shouted. It's the only word with five letters in the wordsquare.

A	B	T	L	P	A	L
S	E	A	I	U	N	O
E	D	L	O	T	S	V
B	O	L	N	Y	W	E
A	R	O	O	M	E	X
N	P	O	W	E	R	E
D	R	I	C	H	E	O

Extra exercises

1 Read the descriptions. Then complete the names of the jobs.

1 I write books.   w*riter*
2 I travel to dangerous places.   e _____
3 My new CD is in the shops now.   s _____
4 I work in a school.   t _____
5 You can see me at the cinema.   a _____
6 I work with wild animals.   z _____

2 These sentences are false. Can you correct them?

1 *He wasn't Spanish. He was English.*
1 Charles Dickens was Spanish.
2 Rembrandt and Goya were explorers.
3 John Lennon was a scientist.
4 Leonardo da Vinci was born in Australia.
5 The Beatles were French.
6 Marilyn Monroe was a painter.

3 Complete the sentences with *was* or *were*.

1 There _____ a snake on my bed this morning.
2 There _____ a dolphin in the bath.
3 There _____ three spiders in my trainers.
4 There _____ two small elephants on the bus.
5 And there _____ a gorilla outside our school.
6 It _____ a very strange morning!

4 Put the words in the right order and make questions about Jane Goodall.

1 was / Jane / where / born ?
2 she / what / love / did ?
3 money / did / her / why / she / save ?
4 she / travel / did / where ?
5 did / what / watch / day / every / she ?

5 Now answer the questions about Jane Goodall in Exercise 4. You can look at the text on page 118 for help.

6 Choose the right word.

1 Van Gogh was a famous _____ .
   a actress
   b painter
   c actor
2 There _____ 10,000 people at the concert.
   a was
   b wasn't
   c were
3 I _____ school when I was six.
   a finished
   b started
   c worked
4 Mozart _____ born in Salzburg.
   a was
   b is
   c were
5 What did Jane Goodall _____ ?
   a studies
   b study
   c studied
6 Lisa _____ on the bus this morning.
   a wasn't
   b were
   c weren't
7 _____ was a spaceship outside our school when I arrived.
   a It
   b There
   c He

7 Give true answers to these questions.

1 Were you happy at primary school?
2 Was the school near your house?
3 Were you interested in geography?
4 Were you good at art?
5 What time did your lessons start?
6 When did they finish?

8 How do you say these sentences in your language?

1 I wasn't happy at first.
2 I'm not so sure now.
3 She was born in Poland.
4 When I was little, I wanted to be a pop star.
5 We were really nervous.

Extra reading

From North to South

Where are the North and South Poles?
What's the weather like there?

Robert Schumann loves travelling to different countries. When he was ten he travelled to the North Pole with his father. First, they travelled by plane to the base camp in Canada. Then they walked for four days to their final destination. The weather at the North Pole was extremely cold. The temperature was -30° Celsius. There was a cold wind and it snowed every day. But Robert and his father were well prepared. They had warm clothes, good walking shoes and expensive sleeping bags. They stayed at the North Pole for four days.

When he was 11, Robert got a mountain bike for his birthday. His father decided it was time to go on another journey – this time to the South Pole on their mountain bikes. Cycling in the snow isn't easy. The South Pole is situated at high altitude, so the atmosphere is very thin. This means that walking and cycling is difficult – especially at -35° Celsius.

After his trip to the South Pole, Robert visited Australia, the Red Sea, Greenland and Spitsbergen. Now he's studying at university. He knows exactly what he's going to do when he leaves. He wants a career in tourism!

ABOUT THE SOUTH POLE

On the 21st July 1883, the temperature in Vostok, Antarctica was −89.2° Celsius.

Task

Answer the questions.

1 How old was Robert when he visited the North Pole?
2 How did Robert and his father travel to Canada?
3 How many days did they stay at the North Pole?
4 When did Robert get a mountain bike?
5 Did Robert and his father walk to the South Pole?
6 How many places did Robert visit after the South Pole?
7 What is Robert doing now?

12 Heroes

STEP 1

In Step 1 you study
- past simple: negatives, questions and short answers
- time expressions

so that you can
- describe things that happened / didn't happen in the past
- write a letter about a past event

1 Presentation *They didn't say hello*

Lisa and Sadie were at a pop concert last night. It was their favourite group, the Brooklyn Boys.

a What can you say about the pictures?

b 🔊 **Close your book and listen. What was the problem?**

Lisa and Sadie are in the school canteen with Jack. He's asking them about the concert. Lisa's in a very bad mood.

JACK: Was the concert good?

SADIE: Yes, it was great.

JACK: Did you enjoy it, Lisa?

LISA: Yes, I did.

JACK: Why are you angry then? What's the matter?

LISA: Well, after the concert we waited outside the theatre – in the rain.

SADIE: We wanted their autographs.

JACK: Did you see them?

SADIE: Yes, we did – for about two seconds!

JACK: Did they talk to you?

LISA: No, they didn't. They didn't wave. They didn't smile. They didn't say hello. They didn't even look at us!

SADIE: They jumped into a big, black car and then they disappeared.

LISA: So we didn't get their autographs. But I don't care.

JACK: But you like the Brooklyn Boys.

LISA: I liked them, Jack. That was yesterday.

c 🔊 **Listen again and follow in your book. Then choose the right words and make true sentences.**

1 There (*was / wasn't*) a pop concert last night.
2 Lisa and Sadie (*enjoyed / didn't enjoy*) the concert.
3 It (*rained / didn't rain*) yesterday.
4 The Brooklyn Boys (*stopped / didn't*) *stop* outside the theatre.
5 They (*talked / didn't talk*) to the fans.
6 Sadie and Lisa (*were / weren't*) pleased.
7 Lisa (*liked / didn't like*) the Brooklyn Boys yesterday, but she doesn't like them today.

2 Key grammar Past simple: questions and short answers

Complete the short answers.

Did	Sadie	enjoy the concert?
	she	get any autographs?

Yes, she _____ .

_____ , she didn't.

We make questions in the past with Did + subject + verb.

G ➔ 6c, f

3 Practice

Choose the right answer to these questions.

1 Did Lisa like the concert?
  a Yes, she does.
  b Yes, he did.
  c Yes, she did.

2 Did Lisa and Sadie wait outside in the rain?
  a Yes, they did.
  b Yes, we did.
  c No, they didn't.

3 Did Jack go to the concert?
  a No, she didn't.
  b No, he didn't.
  c Yes, he did.

4 Did you see the Brooklyn Boys last night?
  a Yes, I did.
  b No, I don't.
  c No, I didn't.

4 Key grammar

Past simple: negative

Complete the explanation.

Lisa They	didn't	talk to them. smile.

We make negative sentences in the past with the subject + _____ + verb.

G ➔ 6b

5 Practice

These sentences are false. Can you correct them?

1 *They didn't stay at home.*

1 Sadie and Lisa stayed at home last night.
2 Sadie didn't enjoy the concert.
3 Lisa talked to the Brooklyn Boys.
4 They said 'Hi! Nice to meet you.'
5 The singers were very friendly.
6 They waved and smiled at their fans.
7 It didn't rain last night.
8 Lisa wasn't angry after the concert.

6 Writing and speaking

a **What about you?** How many of these things did you do last night? Write six true sentences.

I didn't wash my hair. I cleaned my teeth.

wash my hair   watch TV   finish my homework
clean my teeth   listen to the radio help with the housework

b Work with a friend. Ask your friend at least three questions.

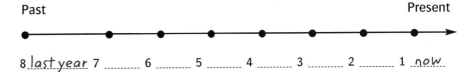

Did you wash your hair last night?   No, I didn't.

7 Key vocabulary *Time expressions*

a Copy the time line. Put the time expressions in the right place.

last year   yesterday afternoon   last night   last week
yesterday morning   now   last month   at the weekend

Past   Present

8 *last year* 7 _____ 6 _____ 5 _____ 4 _____ 3 _____ 2 _____ 1 *now*

🔊 Listen and check.

b Answer the questions.

1 What day was it yesterday?
2 What month was it last month?
3 How old were you on 1st December last year?
4 What did you study in English last week?
5 Did it rain at the weekend?

8 Writing *An angry letter*

Use what you know

Imagine you're Lisa. You're very angry. Write a letter to the Brooklyn Boys.

Dear Brooklyn Boys,
I ... at your concert in Exeter last night. After the concert we ... . But you didn't ... . You ... .
... you care? No, you ...! We ... your fans, but we aren't now!
From
Lisa Carter

In Step 2 you study
- past simple: irregular verbs

so that you can
- describe events in the past

1 Presentation *I went to America*

On September 16th, 1620, a group of 110 English people left Plymouth in the southwest of England and went to America. They were called 'The Pilgrim Fathers'. In the group there was a young boy called John Stockwell. This is John's story.

a Can you put the pictures in the right order?

b 🔊 Listen and follow the text in your book. Then match paragraphs 1–6 with pictures a–f.

c Match the questions with the answers.

1	When did John leave England?	a	Very cold.
2	Where did he and his family go?	b	Local native Americans.
3	Was their journey difficult?	c	Yes, it was.
4	What was the weather like during the winter?	d	No, they didn't.
5	At first, did they have a lot to eat?	e	To America.
6	Did John's sister survive?	f	When he was 12.
7	Who helped them?	g	No, she didn't. She died.

2 Key grammar
Past simple: irregular verbs

Look at the story again. Then complete the table.

Infinitive	Past simple
be	was/were
Regular	
arrive	1 ....
die	died
Irregular	
leave	2 ....
go	went
come	3 ....
see	saw
speak	4 ....
know	5 ....
have	6 ....
eat	ate

G → 7a

1 I was born in Plymouth, in the southwest of England, in 1608. When I was 12, our family left England. We wanted to start a new life and we went to America on a ship called the *Mayflower*.

2 Our journey across the Atlantic wasn't easy. After nine weeks, we arrived on the east coast of America, at a place we called Plymouth!

3 The weather was very cold and our first winter was long and difficult. We were often hungry and a lot of people didn't survive. My sister Mary died and my father was very ill.

4 One day in March, a native American came to Plymouth. We were scared when we saw him, but he was kind and friendly, and he spoke English. His name was Squanto.

5 We didn't know how to find food. But Squanto knew everything. He and his friends helped us. They saved our lives.

6 Soon we had corn, fruit and vegetables. We ate fish and meat, and at last we weren't hungry.

This was the beginning of the USA, and a native American Indian was the hero.

3 Practice

a Use verbs from the table in Exercise 2 and complete the sentences about the story.

1 John ..*left*.. England when he ..*was*.. 12.
2 He and his family .... to a new country.
3 In March, Squanto .... to John's new home.
4 Squanto .... a native American but he .... English.
5 John .... scared when he .... Squanto.
6 Squanto .... how to find food.
7 Soon the Pilgrims .... more food.
8 They .... fruit, vegetables, fish and meat.

b Test a friend Write at least one sentence using an irregular past verb. Leave a space for the verb. Can your friend complete the sentence?

I .... to a football match last Saturday.

4 Key grammar

Irregular verbs: negative and questions

Complete the table.

Affirmative: They knew. They went.
Negative: They didn't know. They .... go.
Questions: Did they know? Did they .... ?

 7b

5 Practice

For each verb make a past simple affirmative and negative sentence and a question.

1 They came. They didn't come. Did they come?

1 come / they
2 see / she
3 eat / we
4 speak / he
5 have / you

6 Writing and speaking

⏱ Think of differences between people today and the Pilgrim Fathers. Work with a friend and make a list. You've got five minutes!

The Pilgrim Fathers didn't have televisions. Their lives were very hard.

7 Listening and speaking

a 📻 **What about you?** Listen to the sentences. Are they true for you? Write *true* or *false*.

b 📻 Listen to the sentences again, then say at least two true things about you.

> I didn't have cereal for my breakfast this morning.

8 Writing *My diary*

Use what you know

Write your diary for last weekend. (Use the list of irregular verbs on page 143.)

On Saturday, I went to my friend's house.

Or

Write about an imaginary day.

On Saturday, I went to the World Cup Final.

STEP 3

In Step 3 you
- read an advert
- listen to a song

so that you can
- talk about holidays
- talk about your school year

GOING TO AUSTRALIA?

Then come with us. We've got the best prices and the best flights.

Sydney € **799**
Perth € **749**
Melbourne € **789**

Book now!
0870 888 456
OPEN 24/7
email sales@jetlineoz.com
or visit www.jetlineoz

Jetline Oz – blink and you're there!

1 Reading *Jetline Oz*

a Read the advert. What is it for?

a train tickets
b hotels in Australia
c plane tickets

b Complete the sentences with words from the advert.

1 .... , ... and .... are three cities in Australia.
2 A ticket to Sydney costs ....
3 You can .... your flight by phone, email or on the Internet.
4 The Jetline Oz office is .... every day.

2 Listening *Song*

a Listen to the song. Where's the singer going? When?

b Match the sentences with the pictures.

1 I finished school.
2 I booked my ticket.
3 I bought some clothes.
4 I packed my bag.
5 I'm flying to Sydney on Sunday.
6 I'm going to swim with the sharks.

a

b

c

d

e

f

c Are the sentences in 2b about the past or the future? Make two lists.

The past: 1, ...   The future: ...

3 Key pronunciation
Words with the same sound

Listen and repeat the words. Find words with the same sound and make three groups.

bag   bought   fun   black
come   walk   lunch short
hand   catch   love   door   hall
month sad   rug   flat   floor

1 bag	2 bought	3 fun
black		

4 Speaking
The past and the future

Use what you know

Think about your first term at secondary school. Share your ideas with the class.

What did you enjoy? What didn't you enjoy? What did you do in your English lessons?

> I like sport, but we didn't do much sport. In our English class, we talked about ...

Now think about your summer holiday. Imagine your ideal summer. What are you going to do?

> I'm going to go to Australia with the boy in the song.

CHAPTER 10

A horse for the king's men

A silver light came from the moonstone in Sophie's hand. Everywhere in the cave there were knights with their white horses. They were all asleep. In the middle of the cave, she saw a man in rich clothes, with a crown on his head.

Then Merlin spoke to her:

'A hundred knights are sleeping here with their king – King Arthur. They're waiting for the day when England is in great danger. Then their mission is to save the country from destruction. But one knight hasn't got a horse. That's why Epona is here. You must leave her. And you must leave the moonstone too. The king needs the stone's power. But he's got a gift for you. It's in this box. Thank you, Sophie. You can go home now.'

Sophie came out of the cave and went along the path. She was alone. She stopped and looked at the hill. It was just an ordinary hill – no gate, no cave …

She opened the box in her hand. Inside, there was a necklace of nine stones with the nine signs of her journey. And there was a piece of paper.

Suddenly the sky changed and the sun disappeared. A great wind came from the north. Sophie fell, and everything went black.

— ● ● ● —

When she opened her eyes, she was in a London taxi. The noise of the traffic filled her ears. The taxi stopped outside her flat. She got out, found her key and went into the flat. On the floor there was a letter …

- Look at the text message in Chapter 9 (page 121). What does the last line mean?

- On the piece of paper in the box there was a poem. Look at the meaning of the signs in chapters 1–9, and find the secrets of the poem.

1 Life is a R,
  A N or a dream.
  You can go alone,
  Or with friends in a M.

2 You're looking for the ⌈,
  But the ⟨ isn't clear.
  Tomorrow is a ⌈,
  Tomorrow isn't here.

3 But there's a F in the wind,
  A voice from the hill.
  The king has got a X for you.
  ⚡, silent ⚡.

- If you have time, use your imagination and continue the story. What happened next? What was in the letter? Who was it from?

Extra exercises

1 Complete the sentences with verbs in the past simple.

1 Our class _visited_ the Science Museum last week. (*visit*)
2 We _____ some very old cars. (*see*)
3 My best friend _____ Arabic when he was little. (*speak*)
4 I'm not hungry. I _____ two pizzas last night. (*eat*)
5 Andy _____ his lunch at Pete's house yesterday. (*have*)
6 We _____ Canada when I _____ two. (*leave, be*)

2 Choose the right word.

1 They _____ to a concert last night.
  a were
  b visited
  c went
2 They didn't _____ any autographs.
  a enjoy
  b get
  c know
3 John wanted to _____ a new life.
  a start
  b stop
  c go
4 I _____ have a bike when I was little.
  a don't
  b didn't
  c do
5 John left England when he _____ 12.
  a was
  b had
  c did
6 Why _____ you at school yesterday?
  a didn't
  b did
  c weren't
7 We _____ fish and chips for our lunch yesterday.
  a had
  b were
  c eat

3 Complete the conversation. Answer the questions about a real or imaginary holiday.

FRIEND: Where did you go?
YOU: ¹_____ .
FRIEND: Who did you go with?
YOU: ²_____ .
FRIEND: Was the food good?
YOU: ³_____ .
FRIEND: What did you eat?
YOU: ⁴_____ .
FRIEND: Did you enjoy your holiday?
YOU: ⁵_____ .

4 These sentences are false. Can you correct them? Use the past simple negative.

1 *The Brooklyn Boys didn't smile at Lisa and Sadie.*

1 The Brooklyn Boys smiled at Lisa and Sadie.
2 Lisa got their autographs.
3 Jack went to the concert.
4 John Stockwell was born in America.
5 His sister, Mary, died in France.
6 At first, the Pilgrim Fathers had a lot of food.

5 Complete the conversations.

1 When did she arrive?
  a Yesterday.
  b Tomorrow.
  c Three months.
2 Did Lisa and Sadie enjoy the concert?
  a No, she didn't.
  b No, we didn't.
  c No, they didn't.
3 What was the weather like yesterday?
  a It's cloudy.
  b It rained.
  c It's going to snow.
4 When did Harry meet Sally?
  a She met him yesterday.
  b Yes, she did.
  c Every day.
5 What did you have for breakfast?
  a At seven o'clock.
  b I had cereal.
  c In the kitchen.

6 How do you say these sentences in your language?

1 Did you enjoy the match?
2 They didn't even smile.
3 I don't care. It isn't important.
4 Why is Lisa in a bad mood?
5 It's the end of the book! At last!

Extra reading

Quiz: The UK and the USA

What do you know about the United Kingdom and the United States of America? Do the quiz and find out.

7 When did America declare independence from Britain?
a 4th July 1776
b 4th July 1946
c 14th July 1776

8 Who was the first female prime minister in Europe?
a Margaret Thatcher
b Margaret Drabble
c Margaret Fletcher

9 In the USA, the President's wife is called:
a The First Woman
b Mrs President
c The First Lady

10 The British flag is called
a The Stars and Stripes
b The Union Jack
c The St. George's Cross

1 How many states are there in the USA?
a 152
b 52
c 50

2 How many countries are there in the UK?
a Four
b Five
c Three

3 What is the capital of the USA?
a New York
b Los Angeles
c Washington

4 Where does the Prime Minister of the UK live?
a 10 Downing Street
b The Houses of Parliament
c Buckingham Palace

5 Where did the first native North Americans come from?
a Europe
b Asia
c Africa

6 When did the Pilgrim Fathers arrive in America?
a 1520
b 1620
c 1720

Now check your answers with your teacher. How many did you get right?

ABOUT THE NATIVE AMERICANS

Some of the early native North Americans greeted people with the words '*Hau kola*'. It means '*Hello, friend*'. The Europeans who went to North America copied this, and '*Hau*' became '*Hi!*'.

Module 6 Review

Language summary

1 Past simple: *was/were*

Present		Past
I am	→	I was
He/She/It is	→	He/She/It was
We/You/They are	→	We/You/They were

Affirmative

I/He/She/It was	sad.
You/We/They were	busy.

Negative

I/He/She/It wasn't	happy.
You/We/They weren't	free.

wasn't = was not	weren't = were not

Questions

Were they		Yes, they were.
	late?	No, they weren't.
Was he/she/it		Yes, he/she/it was.
		No, he/she/it wasn't

Where	was he?
	were they?

Check that you can

1.1 ● talk about the past, using *be*.

A policeman is asking a man questions. Complete and practise the conversation.

A: Where .... you <u>at eleven o'clock last night</u>?

B: I .... <u>at the Kularoo Club</u>.

A: .... , you weren't.

B: .... , I was. Ask <u>my girlfriend</u>. She .... with me.

Make another conversation. Change the <u>underlined</u> words.

1.2 ● make questions with *was* and *were*.

1 *Where was the Colossus?*

1 Where / the Colossus ?

2 Where / Cleopatra's palace ?

3 Who / Julius Caesar ?

4 Who / the Marx Brothers ?

5 What / Apollo 11 ?

6 When / the first Olympic Games ?

Do you know the answers?

2 There was/were

We use *there was* with singular nouns and *there were* with plural nouns.

> *Affirmative*
> There was a gym at Ben's primary school.
> There were two hamsters.
>
> *Negative*
> There wasn't a swimming pool.
> There weren't any tennis courts.
>
> *Questions and short answers*
> Was there a library?
> Yes, there was. / No, there wasn't.
> Were there any English books?
> Yes, there were. / No, there weren't.

Check that you can

● use the different forms of *there was/were*.

Complete the questions about your primary school and make true answers.

1 *Were there any computers?*
  Yes, there were.

1 .... any computers?

2 .... any computer games?

3 .... a canteen?

4 .... a library?

5 .... any English books?

6 .... any pets?

7 .... a lot of pupils?

3 Past simple: regular and irregular verbs

Verbs in the past simple can be 'regular' or 'irregular'. Regular verbs end in -ed; irregular verbs are all different! The form is the same for *I, you, he, she, it, we, they.*

I You He She	*Regular* enjoyed the concert. washed the car.
We You They	*Irregular* went to Timbuktu. saw a gorilla.

We form the negative and questions in the same way for regular and irregular verbs.

I You He She We You They	didn't	*Regular* enjoy the concert. wash the car.
		Irregular go to Timbuktu. see a gorilla.

Questions

Did	you	enjoy the concert?
	he/she	see any gorillas?
Yes, I/he/she/we did. No, I/he/she/we didn't.		

Where did	she	live?
	they	go?

See Spelling notes, page 142.

Check that you can

3.1 ● describe things that happened in the past.

Complete the sentences. Put the verbs in the list in the simple past.

go   visit   watch   believe   see   want   eat

When Ben was little:

1 he __saw__ a UFO from his bedroom window.
2 he _____ in Father Christmas.
3 he _____ to a primary school in Exeter.
4 he _____ a lot of cartoons on TV.
5 he _____ two banana yoghurts a day.
6 he _____ his relatives in Canada.
7 he _____ to be a pilot.

3.2 ● describe things that didn't happen in the past.

Look at the sentences about Ben and write true sentences about you.

1 *I didn't see a UFO when I was little.*

3.3 ● ask questions about the past.

Put the words in the right order and make questions.

1 Jane / England / leave / did / when ?
2 go / Africa / did / to / she / why ?
3 Jack / live / where / did ?
4 native Americans / the / did / the / help / Pilgrims ?
5 they / language / did / what / speak ?
6 Lisa / did / the / enjoy / concert ?

4 Time expressions

Time expressions tell us when something happened.

Our bus was late I packed my bag They left	this morning. last night. yesterday. yesterday afternoon. at the weekend. last week/month/year.

Check that you can

● say when something happened.

Make at least three true sentences using the time expressions in the table.

I went to bed at ten o'clock last night.

5 Past simple of *have / have got*

The past simple form of *have* and *have got* is *had*:
***I've got** a bike.* → ***I had** a bike when I was five.*
***I have** my lunch in the canteen every day.*
→ ***I had** my lunch in the canteen yesterday.*

Check that you can

● use *have got* and *have* in the past.

Rewrite the sentences using *yesterday*.

1 *I had a shower yesterday.*

1 I have a shower every day.
2 I've got a cold today.
3 I have sandwiches for lunch every day.
4 The Kellys always have their dinner at eight.
5 Lee has got a headache.

Vocabulary

Occupations

actor
actress
doctor
explorer
film star
nurse
painter
pilot
pop star
scientist
singer
teacher
writer
zoologist

At primary school

best friend
library
little
Sports Day
(to) start school

Holidays

(to) go away
(to) pack (a bag)
ticket
(to) travel

Irregular past verbs

ate (eat)
bought (buy)
came (come)
had (have got/ have)
knew (know)
left (leave)
saw (see)
spoke (speak)
went (go)
(*See Irregular verbs, page 143.*)

Time expressions

at the weekend
last month
last night
last week
last year
yesterday
yesterday afternoon
yesterday morning

Expressions

At first, ...
At last, ...
I don't care.
in a bad mood
I'm not so sure.

Study skills 6   Planning your learning

What can you do in the future to improve your English? Read the list, then choose at least one thing. Tell the class.

> I'm going to try to read some English magazines.

- start a vocabulary notebook
- make at least four vocabulary cards every week
- try to read some English magazines
- talk to the cat in English
- try to talk to the teacher in English
- greet my friends in English at the beginning and end of the lesson
- concentrate more in class

How's it going?

- ## Your rating

Look again at pages 132–133. For each section give yourself a star rating:

Good ☆ ☆ ☆   Not bad ☆ ☆   I can't remember much ☆

- ## Vocabulary

Choose five words from the Vocabulary list and write a sentence for each word.

- ## Test a friend

Look again at Units 11 and 12. Think of at least two questions, then ask a friend.

> Who was Albert Einstein?
> What happened to John Stockwell's sister?

- ## Write to your teacher

It's the end of the book! Write a final letter to your teacher in your own language.

- ## Your Workbook

Complete the Learning diaries for Units 11 and 12.

Coursework 6 – All about me!

Read about Jack. Then make a 'life line'. Write about important events in your life and put your age. Use pictures, drawings and photos too.

My life line

Age 0   I was born at the Manchester Royal Infirmary on 2nd October.

Age 4½   I started primary school.

Age 6   I was in the nativity play at school at Christmas. I learnt how to swim.

Age 7   My first visit to London. We went on the London Eye.

Age 8   We bought my first bike.

Age 9   My mum and I went to Spain on holiday.

Age 10   I won the first prize in an art competition.

Age 11   My granddad died. We moved to Exeter. I started at Westover Comprehensive School.

Age 12   I joined Friends of the Earth. Our class went camping on Dartmoor.

1st prize awarded to Jack Ellis, aged 10

CHOO CHOO I love trains
Friends of the Earth

Wild about wildlife
Friends of the Earth

Grammar index

	Unit/Step	Review	Workbook Grammar notes
A and An I've got a scarf and an anorak.	3.1	2	15
Adjectives She's got long dark curly hair.	4.1, 4.2, 4.3	2	22
Be			
● present simple Sadie is English.	2.1, 2.2	1	2
● past simple Joe wasn't at school yesterday.	11.1	6	3
Can			
● ability I can swim.	8.1	4	12
● possibility You can buy CDs here.	8.2	4	12
● with see, hear I can hear music.	8.2	4	12
● permission Can I use your computer?	1.3	1, 4	12
Countable nouns a boy two boys	7.2	4	18
Frequency adverbs (always, usually, often, sometimes, never)			
She often eats fish.	6.1	3	23
Future: going to I'm going to be a pop star.	10.2	5	8
Have I usually have sandwiches for lunch.	6.2	3	10
Have got They've got a dog called Sam.	3.1, 4.3	2, 3	10
Sadie has got a tortoise.	3.1, 4.2,	2, 3	10
Imperative Listen! Don't talk!	8.3	4	9
Must I must go home now.	8.3	4	13
Object pronouns (me, you, him, her, it, us, them) Everyone's looking at me.	9.2	5	25
Past simple			
● regular verbs I watched TV last night.	11.2, 11.3, 12.1	6	6
● irregular verbs She went to London yesterday.	12.1, 12.2	6	7
Plural nouns river → rivers, city → cities	2.3, 3.1	1	17
Possessive adjectives (my, your, his, her, our, their) This is my room.	3.2	2	21
Prepositions			
● place There's a poster on the wall.	7.3	1, 4	24
● time I'm playing tennis on Saturday.	2.1	1	24
Present continuous			
● to describe the present It's raining.	9.1, 9.2	5	4
● with future meaning I'm seeing Kim tomorrow.	10.1	5	4
Present simple He works in a shop.	5.1, 5.2, 5.3 6.1	3, 5	5
Question words (What, Where, etc.) What's your name?	2.1, 5.3, 11.3	1	14
Possessive 's Lisa is Sadie's best friend.	3.2	2	20
Some and any We've got some eggs. We haven't got any tomatoes.	3.1	2	19
Subject pronouns (I, you, he, she, it, we, they) I'm twelve and he's eleven.	1.2, 2.1		1
Suggestions (Let's ...?, Shall we ...?, Why don't we ...?) Shall we dance?	10.1	5	26
There is/are There's a cinema and there are two cafés.	7.1	4	11
There was a good film on last night.	11.1	6	11
This/these, that/those This is my pen. That's Sadie's pen.	3.2	2	16
Uncountable nouns We need some bread and some milk.	7.2	4	18

Communicative functions index

Unit 1

- Introduce yourself
  My name's Danny.
- Ask for help in the classroom
  What does ... mean?
  How do you spell ... ?
- Ask for and give personal
  information   *What's your phone
  number? I live in Exeter.*
- Count from one to a hundred
  One, two, three ...
- Use the English alphabet
  A, B, C ...
- Say the date
  It's the sixth of March.
- Ask for permission
  Can I open the window, please?
- Ask for help   *Can you help me?*
- Greet people in English and say
  goodbye   *Hello. How are you?*
  Goodbye. See you tomorrow.
- Understand and write a simple
  letter in English

Unit 2

- Ask questions with *What, Where,*
  etc. *Where's Sam?*
- Talk about your interests and
  activities   *I'm quite good at
  sport. I'm interested in animals.*
- Talk about places around the
  world   *Washington is the capital
  of the USA.*

Unit 3

- Describe common objects
  key, watch, calculator
- Talk about your possessions
  I've got a CD player.
- Identify things   *This is my
  lunchbox. That's your lunchbox.*
- Say that something belongs to
  someone   *It's Joe's mobile
  phone.*
- Talk about families   *I've got five
  cousins.*

Unit 4

- Ask for a description   *What's it
  like? / What are they like?*
- Describe things   *It's a really
  brilliant video.*
- Describe a person's appearance
  *He's tall and he's got straight
  hair.*
- Describe a person's personality
  He's a kind, honest man.
- Say how you feel   *I'm tired and
  I've got a headache.*

Unit 5

- Talk about things you do
  regularly   *I play the piano.
  I wear trainers.*
- Talk about your likes and dislikes
  *I like computers. I don't like
  mushrooms.*
- Talk about fears   *I'm scared of
  the dark.*
- Ask and answer questions about
  daily life   *Where do you come
  from? Do you live in a flat?*

Unit 6

- Talk about habits and routines
  *Dolphins live in groups.
  I sometimes help at home.*
- Talk about things you eat and
  drink   *I like chicken. We often
  have pasta for dinner.*
- Tell the time   *It's half past
  eight.*
- Say when you do things
  I get up at seven o'clock.

Unit 7

- Describe different homes
  *There's a living room but there
  isn't a dining room.*
- Ask about places   *Is there a
  television here?*
- Ask about food   *Is there any
  fruit juice?*
- Say where things are   *The lamp
  is on the table.*
- Describe a room   *The bed is
  in the corner, next to the desk.*

Unit 8

- Describe your abilities
  I can swim but I can't ski.
- Talk about things you can do in
  your town   *You can visit the
  museum.*
- Describe the sounds and sights
  around you   *I can hear a plane.
  I can see the river.*
- Talk about obligations
  *You must tidy your room.
  I must do my homework.*
- Tell people what to do   *Be quiet!
  Don't go!*

Unit 9

- Talk about actions in progress
  *A billion people are watching
  football on TV.*
- Describe your clothes   *I usually
  wear jeans and a T-shirt.*

Unit 10

- Talk about future arrangements
  I'm meeting Rick at five o'clock.
- Make suggestions   *Let's go
  swimming. Shall we play
  volleyball? Why don't we ask Joe?*
- Respond to a suggestion   *OK.
  That's fine. Sorry, but I can't.*
- Talk about plans and intentions
  He's going to take some photos.
- Talk about the weather   *It's hot
  and sunny.*
- Write a holiday postcard

Unit 11

- Talk about people from the past
  *Einstein was a scientist. The
  Beatles were British.*
- Say what happened in the past
  *Jane Goodall lived in Africa. She
  studied chimpanzees.*
- Describe your early childhood
  I didn't like school.

Unit 12

- Write a description of events in
  the past   *I saw a great film last
  Saturday.*

Wordlist

A

a lot of /ə lɒt əv/ 4.1
about (something) /əˈbaʊt/ 2.1
about (= approximately)
   /əˈbaʊt/ 6.1
above /əˈbʌv/ 5.2
accept /əkˈsept/ 11.2
across /əˈkrɒs/ 5.2
actor /ˈæktə/ 11.1
actress /ˈæktrəs/ 11.1
addict /ˈædɪkt/ 5.1
address /əˈdres/ 1.2
adult /ˈædʌlt/ 5.1
aeroplane /ˈeərəpleɪn/ 11.3
after /ˈɑːftə/ 8.3
afternoon /ˌɑːftəˈnuːn/ 10.3
again /əˈgen/ 9.2
age /eɪdʒ/ 6.SP
aged /eɪdʒd/ 4.1
alien /ˈeɪliən/ 5.2
(we're) all (students) /ɔːl/ 2.1
all over /ɔːl ˈəʊvə/ 9.1
(I'm) all right /ɔːl raɪt/ 1.3
alone /əˈləʊn/ 8.SP
(go) along /əˈlɒŋ/ 12.SP
always /ˈɔːlweɪz/ 6.1
amazing /əˈmeɪzɪŋ/ 8.2
ambition /æmˈbɪʃn/ 11.2
angry /ˈæŋgri/ 12.1
animal /ˈænɪml/ 1.1
announce /əˈnaʊnts/ 3.3
anorak /ˈænəræk/ 3.1
another /əˈnʌðə/ 2.1
anyway /ˈeniweɪ/ 7.2
apartment /əˈpɑːtmənt/ 7.1
appear /əˈpɪə/ 11.SP
apple /ˈæpl/ 1.1
aquarium /əˈkweəriəm/ 8.2
argue /ˈɑːgjuː/ 8.3
arm /ɑːm/ 4.1
arrive /əˈraɪv/ 11.2
art /ɑːt/ 2.2
article (magazine) /ˈɑːtɪkl/ 2.1
as usual /əz ˈjuːʒl/ 9.1
ask /ɑːsk/ 1.2
asleep /əˈsliːp/ 9.1
at first /ət ˈfɜːst/ 11.2
at home /ət həʊm/ 6.2
at last /ət lɑːst/ 12.2
attack (v) /əˈtæk/ 5.2
aunt /ɑːnt/ 3.3
autograph (n) /ˈɔːtəgrɑːf/ 12.1
awful /ˈɔːfl/ 4.1

B

baby /ˈbeɪbi/ 3.3
bad /bæd/ 2.2
badge /bædʒ/ 3.1
badger /ˈbædʒə/ CW2
bag /bæg/ 1.1
balcony /ˈbælkəni/ 10.3
ball /bɔːl/ 9.2
banana /bəˈnɑːnə/ 1.1
band /bænd/ 1.2
baseball cap
   /ˈbeɪsbɔːl kæp/ 3.1
basketball /ˈbɑːskɪtbɔːl/ 5.1
bass guitarist
   /beɪs gɪˈtɑːrɪst/ 2.1
bat /bæt/ 5.2
bathroom /ˈbɑːθrʊm/ 7.1
beach /biːtʃ/ 2.2
Be careful! /bi: ˈkeəfl/ 3.SP
bear (n) /beə/ 6.1
beat (n) /biːt/ 2.3
because /bɪˈkɒz/ 1.2
become /bɪˈkʌm/ 4.2
bed /bed/ 4.SP
bedroom /ˈbedrʊm/ 7.1
begin /bɪˈgɪn/ 8.2
beginning /bɪˈgɪnɪŋ/ 12.2
behind /bɪˈhaɪnd/ 7.3
believe /bɪˈliːv/ 5.2
belong to /bɪˈlɒŋ tuː/ 8.SP
belt /belt/ 9.3
best wishes /best ˈwɪʃɪz/ 1.2
big /bɪg/ 4.1
bike /baɪk/ 1.1
binoculars /bɪˈnɒkjələz/ 11.2
biology /baɪˈɒlədʒi/ CW3
bird /bɜːd/ 8.1
birth /bɜːθ/ 3.3
birthday /ˈbɜːθdeɪ/ 2.1
blink /blɪŋk/ 6.1
body /ˈbɒdi/ 4.3
book (n) /bʊk/ 4.1
book (v) /bʊk/ 12.3
boot /buːt/ 9.3
bored /bɔːd/ 6.1
boring /ˈbɔːrɪŋ/ 4.1
(be) born /bɔːn/ 11.1
both /bəʊθ/ 5.1
bottle /ˈbɒtl/ 1.1
bowling alley /ˈbəʊlɪŋ ˈæli/ 8.2
box /bɒx/ 12.SP
boyfriend /ˈbɔɪfrend/ 2.2
bread /bred/ 6.2

break (n) /breɪk/ CW3
breakfast /ˈbrekfəst/ 6.2
bridge /brɪdʒ/ 8.SP
brilliant /ˈbrɪliənt/ 2.1
brochure /ˈbrəʊʃə/ 10.2
brother /ˈbrʌðə/ 1.2
building /ˈbɪldɪŋ/ 8.2
bus pass /bʌs pɑːs/ CW3
bus station /bʌs ˈsteɪʃn/ 8.2
bus stop /bʌs stɒp/ 2.2
busy /ˈbɪzi/ 10.1
but /bʌt/ 2.1
butter /ˈbʌtə/ 6.2
buy /baɪ/ 7.2
by (someone) /baɪ/ 2.1
by (= next to) /baɪ/ 7.1
Bye. /baɪ/ 1.3

C

CD player /ˌsiːˈdiː ˈpleɪə/ 3.1
café /ˈkæfeɪ/ 8.2
calculator /ˈkælkjəleɪtə/ 3.1
call (v) /kɔːl/ 10.SP
(be) called /kɔːld/ 1.2
camera /ˈkæmərə/ 1.1
camping /kæmpɪŋ/ CW6
can (n) /kæn/ 4.1
canteen /kænˈtiːn/ 6.2
capital /ˈkæpɪtl/ 2.2
car /kɑːr/ 2.2
care /keə/ 12.1
carry /ˈkæri/ 9.3
cartoon /kɑːˈtuːn/ 11.3
cat /kæt/ 1.1
catch (the bus) /kætʃ/ 6.3
cathedral /kəˈθiːdrəl/ 8.2
cave /keɪv/ 9.SP
cereal /ˈsɪəriəl/ 6.2
chair /tʃeə/ 7.3
champion /ˈtʃæmpiən/ 6.3
change (v) /tʃeɪndʒ/ 9.SP
cheese /tʃiːz/ 6.2
chemistry /ˈkemɪstri/ 9.2
chest of drawers /tʃest əv
   drɔːz/ 7.3
chicken /ˈtʃɪkɪn/ 6.2
child (pl children) /tʃaɪld/ 3.3
childhood /ˈtʃaɪldhʊd/ 11.3
chimpanzee /ˌtʃɪmpənˈziː/ 11.2
chips /tʃɪps/ 5.1
choose /tʃuːz/ 6.1
church /tʃɜːtʃ/ 8.2
cinema /ˈsɪnəmə/ 3.1
circle (n) /ˈsɜːkl/ 6.SP

city /ˈsɪti/ 2.3
clap /klæp/ 2.3
classroom /ˈklɑːsrʊm/ 1.1
clean (v) /kliːn/ 6.1
cloak /kləʊk/ 11.SP
clock /klɒk/ 7.3
close (v) /kləʊz/ 1.3
clothes /kləʊðz/ 9.3
cloudy /ˈklaʊdi/ 10.3
club /klʌb/ 5.1
coast /kəʊst/ 8.1
coat /kəʊt/ 9.3
coffee /ˈkɒfi/ 5.1
cold /kəʊld/ 10.3
(I've got a) cold /kəʊld/ 4.3
come /kʌm/ 2.1
come in /kʌm ɪn/ 7.2
Come on! /kʌm ɒn/ 3.2
comfortable /ˈkʌmftəbl/ CW5
comic /ˈkɒmɪk/ 5.2
(film) company
   /ˈkʌmpəni/ 11.2
competition /ˌkɒmpəˈtɪʃn/ 8.1
competitor /kəmˈpetɪtə/ 8.1
computer /kəmˈpjuːtə/ 1.1
concert /ˈkɒnsət/ 10.3
contact /ˈkɒntækt/ 2.1
cook (v) /kʊk/ 8.1
cooking /ˈkʊkɪŋ/ 2.2
corn /kɔːn/ 12.2
(in the) corner /ˈkɔːnə/ 7.3
cost (v) /kɒst/ 12.3
cottage /ˈkɒtɪdʒ/ 3.SP
country /ˈkʌntri/ 2.3
cousin /ˈkʌzn/ 2.2
crazy /ˈkreɪzi/ 8.1
crisps /krɪsps/ 3.1
crown /kraʊn/ 12.SP
cruel /ˈkruːəl/ 4.2
cup /kʌp/ 10.2
cupboard /ˈkʌbəd/ 8.2
curly /ˈkɜːli/ 4.2
curry /ˈkʌri/ 6.2

D

dad /dæd/ 3.2
dance /dɑːnts/ 8.1
dancer /ˈdɑːntsə/ 4.1
dangerous /ˈdeɪndʒərəs/ 4.1
dark (adj) /dɑːk/ 4.2
dark (n) /dɑːk/ 5.2
date /deɪt/ 1.3
daughter /ˈdɔːtə/ 3.3

day /deɪ/ 1.1
dear /dɪə/ 1.3
dentist /'dentɪst/ 10.1
desk /desk/ 1.1
destroy /dɪ'strɔɪ/ 9.SP
devil /'devl/ 8.SP
diary /'daɪəri/ 12.2
dictionary /'dɪkʃənri/ 1.2
die /daɪ/ 12.2
different /'dɪfrənt/ 4.2
difficult /'dɪfɪkəlt/ 4.1
dining room /'daɪnɪŋ ruːm/ 7.1
dinner /'dɪnə/ 6.2
dinosaur /'daɪnəsɔː/ 10.2
disappear /,dɪsə'pɪə/ 11.SP
disgusting /dɪs'gʌstɪŋ/ 7.2
dive /daɪv/ 8.1
divided /dɪ'vaɪdɪd/ 9.1
diving /'daɪvɪŋ/ 6.3
do /duː/ 6.1
doctor /'dɒktə/ 4.2
dog /dɒg/ 1.2
dolphin /'dɒlfɪn/ 6.1
Don't panic!
    /dəʊnt 'pænɪk/ 1.2
Don't worry. /dəʊnt 'wʌri/ 4.SP
door /dɔː/ 4.SP
double /'dʌbl/ 1.3
downstairs /,daʊn'steəz/ 7.1
draw /drɔː/ 8.1
dream (n) /driːm/ 4.SP
dream (adj) /driːm/ 7.1
dream (v) /driːm/ 9.2
dress /dres/ 4.SP
drink (v) /drɪŋk/ 5.1
drink (n) /drɪŋk/ 5.3
drummer /'drʌmə/ 2.1
during /'djʊərɪŋ/ 12.2

E

ear /ɪə/ 4.3
east /iːst/ 12.2
easy /'iːzi/ 4.1
eat /iːt/ 3.2
egg /eg/ 6.2
elephant /'elɪfənt/ 1.1
email (n) /'iːmeɪl/ 2.1
empty /'empti/ 4.3
end (n) /end/ 7.SP
energetic /,enə'dʒetɪk/ 6.1
enjoy /ɪn'dʒɔɪ/ 4.1
(that's) enough /ɪ'nʌf/ 8.3
entrance hall
    /'entrəns hɔːl/ 10.2
even /'iːvən/ 12.1
evening /'iːvənɪŋ/ 6.1
every (day) /'evri/ 5.1
everyone /'evriwʌn/ 2.1
everything /'evriθɪŋ/ 5.1
everywhere /'evriweə/ 12.SP

(for) example /ɪg'zɑːmpl/ 4.1
exciting /ɪk'saɪtɪŋ/ 2.1
Excuse me. /ɪk'skjuːs miː/ 6.2
expensive /'ɪkspensɪv/ CW5
explorer /ɪk'splɔːrə/ 11.1
explosion /ɪk'spləʊʒn/ 11.SP
eye /aɪ/ 4.2

F

face /feɪs/ 4.2
fair /feə/ 4.2
faith /feɪθ/ 5.2
fall /fɔːl/ 12.SP
false /fɔːls/ 5.1
family /'fæməli/ 3.3
famous /'feɪməs/ 3.2
fan /fæn/ 9.2
fancy /'fæntsi/ 7.2
fantastic /fæn'tæstɪk/ 2.2
father /'fɑːðə/ 3.2
favourite /'feɪvərɪt/ 2.1
fed up /,fed'ʌp/ 4.3
feel /fiːl/ 8.SP
feet /fiːt/ 2.3
fill /fɪl/ 11.SP
film /fɪlm/ 4.1
final /'faɪnl/ 9.1
find /faɪnd/ 9.2
fine /faɪn/ 1.1
finish /'fɪnɪʃ/ 8.3
fish /fɪʃ/ 6.1
fizzy /'fɪzi/ 10.2
flash /flæʃ/ 8.SP
flat /flæt/ 5.3
floor /flɔːʳ/ 5.2
(the third) floor /flɔːʳ/ 7.1
fly (v) /flaɪ/ 8.1
fly (n) /flaɪ/ 8.1
foggy /'fɒgi/ 10.3
follow /'fɒləʊ/ 8.SP
food /fuːd/ 1.1
foot /fʊt/ 4.3
football /'fʊtbɔːl/ 2.1
footballer /'fʊtbɔːlə/ 2.3
for /fɔː/ 3.2
foreign /'fɒrɪn/ 5.1
forest /'fɒrɪst/ 11.2
fossil /'fɒsl/ 10.2
free /friː/ 6.2
friend /frend/ 2.1
friendly /'frendli/ 4.2
frog /frɒg/ 8.1
(it's) from /frɒm/ 1.2
fruit /fruːt/ 6.2
fruit juice /fruːt dʒuːs/ 6.2
funny /'fʌni/ 4.1

G

game /geɪm/ 2.2
garden /'gɑːdn/ 4.SP

gate /geɪt/ 10.SP
generally /'dʒenərəli/ 6.1
geography /dʒi'ɒgrəfi/ 2.2
get (= to obtain) /get/ 8.1
get home /get həʊm/ 6.1
get out /get aʊt/ 12.SP
get some exercise /get səm
    'eksəsaɪz/ 6.1
get up /get ʌp/ 6.3
ghost /gəʊst/ 5.2
gift /gɪft/ 5.SP
giraffe /dʒɪ'rɑːf/ 6.1
girl /gɜːl/ 5.2
give /gɪv/ 7.SP
glass /glɑːs/ 5.2
glasses /'glɑːsɪz/ 4.2
gloves /glʌvz/ 9.3
go /gəʊ/ 5.1
go back /gəʊ bæk/ 8.SP
go bowling /gəʊ 'bəʊlɪŋ/ 8.2
go for (a walk/swim)
    /gəʊ fə/ 8.2
goal /gəʊl/ 9.1
good /gʊd/ 4.1
(I'm) good at /gʊd ət/ 2.2
Good luck! /gʊd lʌk/ 10.SP
gorilla /gə'rɪlə/ 6.1
grandfather
    /'grænd,fɑːðə/ 3.3
grandmother
    /'grænd,mʌðə/ 3.3
grandparents
    /'grænd,peərənts/ 10.1
graphics /'græfɪks/ 4.1
great /greɪt/ 1.3
ground /graʊnd/ 5.2
group /gruːp/ 2.1
guess /ges/ 1.2
guide /gaɪd/ 4.SP
guitar /gɪ'tɑː/ 5.1
guitarist /gɪ'tɑːrɪst/ 2.1
gym /dʒɪm/ 7.1

H

hair /heə/ 4.2
half /hɑːf/ 6.3
hall /hɔːl/ 7.1
ham /hæm/ 6.2
hamster /'hæmpstə/ 1.3
hand /hænd/ 2.3
Hang on a minute! /hæŋ ɒn ə
    mɪnɪt/ 9.1
happen /'hæpən/ 10.SP
happiness /'hæpɪnəs/ 4.1
happy /'hæpi/ 4.1
hat /hæt/ 9.3
hate /heɪt/ 11.3
have (= eat) /hæv/ 6.2
Have a nice day! 3.2
head /hed/ 4.3

(I've got a) headache
    /'hedeɪk/ 4.3
hear /hɪə/ 3.2
heart /hɑːt/ 4.2
heavy /'hevi/ 4.3
height /haɪt/ 4.2
heights /haɪts/ 5.2
Hello. /hel'əʊ/ 1.1
help /help/ 1.2
helpful /'helpfl/ 6.1
here /'hɪə/ 3.SP
Here you are. 3.1
hero /'hɪərəʊ/ 12.2
Hi. /haɪ/ 1.1
hill /hɪl/ 2.3
history /'hɪstri/ 5.1
hockey /'hɒki/ 5.1
hole /həʊl/ 6.1
holiday /'hɒlədeɪ/ 5.2
home /həʊm/ 5.SP
homework /'həʊmwɜːk/ 1.3
honest /'ɒnɪst/ 4.2
horrible /'hɒrɪbl/ 9.2
horror story /'hɒrə 'stɔːri/ 5.1
horse /hɔːs/ 3.SP
hospital /'hɒspɪtəl/ 3.3
hot /hɒt/ 5.2
hour /aʊə/ 8.SP
house /haʊs/ 3.2
houseboat /'haʊsbəʊt/ 7.1
housework /'haʊswɜːk/ 6.1
How are you? 1.3
How old are you? 1.2
(I'm) hungry /'hʌŋgri/ 3.1
(in a) hurry /'hʌri/ 3.2
Hurry up! /'hʌri ʌp/ 3.2
husband /'hʌzbənd/ 3.3

I

ice cream /,aɪs 'kriːm/ 7.2
idea /aɪ'dɪə/ 10.2
ill /ɪl/ 12.2
important /ɪm'pɔːtnt/ 5.SP
in front of /ɪn frʌnt əv/ 7.3
information /,ɪnfə'meɪʃn/ 8.1
ingredients /ɪn'griːdiənts/ 4.1
insect /'ɪnsekt/ 5.2
inside /,ɪn'saɪd/ 11.SP
instructions /ɪn'strʌkʃnz/ 4.1
intelligent /ɪn'telɪdʒənt/ 6.1
(I'm) interested in
    /'ɪntrəstɪd ɪn/ 1.2
interesting /'ɪntrəstɪŋ/ 8.2
international /,ɪntə'næʃnəl/ 8.1
Internet /'ɪntənet/ 6.1
interrupt /,ɪntə'rʌpt/ 8.3
It depends. /ɪt dɪ'pendz/ 5.2

J

jacket /ˈdʒækɪt/ 9.3
jeans /dʒiːnz/ 9.3
job /dʒɒb/ 10.2
join /dʒɔɪn/ 8.1
journey /ˈdʒɜːni/ 4.SP
judo /ˈdʒuːdəʊ/ 5.1
jump /dʒʌmp/ 12.1
jungle /ˈdʒʌŋgl/ 11.2

K

key /kiː/ 3.1
keyboard /ˈkiːbɔːd/ 2.1
keyboard player /ˈkiːbɔːd ˈpleɪə/ 2.1
kill /kɪl/ 6.1
kind /kaɪnd/ 4.2
king /kɪŋ/ 10.SP
kitchen /ˈkɪtʃɪn/ 3.2
knight /naɪt/ 12.SP
know /nəʊ/ 1.2

L

lake /leɪk/ 2.3
lamp /læmp/ 7.3
last (night) /lɑːst/ 12.1
late /leɪt/ 2.1
lazy /ˈleɪzi/ 6.1
lead guitarist /liːd gɪˈtɑːrɪst/ 2.1
leader /ˈliːdə/ 2.1
learn /lɜːn/ 11.2
leave /liːv/ 6.3
(on the) left /left/ 3.2
leg /leg/ 4.1
lemonade /ˌleməˈneɪd/ 4.1
lesson /ˈlesn/ 10.1
Let's see. /lets siː/ 7.2
letter /ˈletə/ 2.2
library /ˈlaɪbrəri/ 11.3
life /laɪf/ 12.2
light /laɪt/ 6.SP
like /laɪk/ 1.1
line /laɪn/ 11.SP
lion /ˈlaɪən/ 6.1
listen (to) /ˈlɪsn/ 9.2
little /ˈlɪtl/ 8.SP
live /lɪv/ 1.2
living room /ˈlɪvɪŋ ruːm/ 7.1
local /ˈləʊkl/ 12.2
locked /lɒkt/ 7.1
long /lɒŋ/ 4.2
look (at) /lʊk/ 2.1
look out of /lʊk aʊt əv/ 8.2
lots of /lɒts əv/ 7.SP
love (v) /lʌv/ 5.1
lunch /lʌntʃ/ 3.2
lunchbox /ˈlʌntʃbɒks/ 3.2

M

magazine /ˌmægəˈziːn/ 2.1
make /meɪk/ 5.2
man /mæn/ 4.2
manager /ˈmænɪdʒə/ 3.1
map /mæp/ 8.2
market /ˈmɑːkɪt/ 10.3
match (n) /mætʃ/ 9.1
maths /mæθs/ 5.1
meal /miːl/ 5.1
mean /miːn/ 1.2
meat /miːt/ 5.1
meet /miːt/ 2.1
meeting /ˈmiːtɪŋ/ 8.SP
melon /ˈmelən/ 9.2
member /ˈmembə/ 2.1
mess /mes/ 8.3
message /ˈmesɪdʒ/ 1.1
messenger /ˈmesɪndʒə/ 4.SP
metre /ˈmiːtə/ 5.2
(in the) middle (of) /ˈmɪdl/ 7.SP
milk /mɪlk/ 6.2
milkshake /ˈmɪlkʃeɪk/ 7.2
mineral water /ˈmɪnərəl ˈwɔːtə/ 10.2
minute /ˈmɪnɪt/ 3.1
mirror /ˈmɪrər/ 5.SP
mission /ˈmɪʃn/ 6.SP
mix /mɪks/ 4.1
mixed (salad) /mɪkst/ 10.2
mobile (phone) /ˈməʊbaɪl/ 3.1
money /ˈmʌni/ 10.2
month /mʌnθ/ 10.1
mood /muːd/ 4.3
more /mɔː/ 8.1
(in the) morning /ˈmɔːnɪŋ/ 2.2
mosquito /mɒsˈkiːtəʊ/ 8.1
most /məʊst/ 7.2
mother /ˈmʌðə/ 3.2
mountain /ˈmaʊntɪn/ 2.3
mouth /maʊθ/ 4.3
move /muːv/ 8.SP
mum /mʌm/ 3.2
museum /mjuːˈziːəm/ 8.2
mushroom /ˈmʌʃrʊm/ 7.1
music /ˈmjuːzɪk/ 1.2
musical instrument /ˈmjuːzɪkl ˈɪntstrəmənt/ 5.1
mystery /ˈmɪstəri/ 9.SP

N

national /ˈnæʃnəl/ 1.3
nationality /ˌnæʃəˈnæləti/ 1.2
nativity play /nəˈtɪvɪti pleɪ/ CW6
natural history /ˈnætʃrəl ˈhɪstri/ 10.2
near /nɪə/ CW1

nearly /ˈnɪəli/ 5.1
necklace /ˈnekləs/ 12.SP
need /niːd/ 2.1
neighbourhood /ˈneɪbəhʊd/ CW4
nervous /ˈnɜːvəs/ 10.SP
never /ˈnevə/ 6.1
Never mind! /ˈnevə maɪnd/ 2.2
new /njuː/ 2.1
next /nekst/ 2.1
next door to /nekst dɔː tə/ 1.2
next to /nekst tə/ 7.3
nice /naɪs/ 2.2
(It's) Nice to see you. 3.3
night /naɪt/ 12.1
noise /nɔɪz/ 12.SP
noisy /ˈnɔɪzi/ 4.1
north /nɔːθ/ 5.2
nose /nəʊz/ 4.2
now /naʊ/ 3.1
nurse /nɜːs/ CW3

O

(four) o'clock /əˈklɒk/ 2.1
octopus /ˈɒktəpəs/ 4.2
of course /əv ˈkɔːs/ 1.3
office /ˈɒfɪs/ 7.1
often /ˈɒfən/ 6.1
Oh dear! /əʊ dɪə/ 2.3
old /əʊld/ 4.1
omelette /ˈɒmlət/ 7.2
onion /ˈʌnjən/ 7.2
on time /ɒn taɪm/ 6.1
only /ˈəʊnli/ 2.1
open (adj) /ˈəʊpən/ 6.1
open (v) /ˈəʊpən/ 8.2
opposite /ˈɒpəzɪt/ 7.3
orange juice /ˈɒrɪndʒ dʒuːs/ 6.2
other /ˈʌðə/ 2.1
outside /ˌaʊtˈsaɪd/ 8.2
over there /ˈəʊvə ðeər/ 1.1

P

PE (physical education) /ˌpiːˈiː/ 6.1
pack (a bag) /pæk/ 12.3
packet /ˈpækɪt/ 6.2
painter /ˈpeɪntə/ 11.1
paper /ˈpeɪpə/ 7.2
Pardon? /ˈpɑːdn/ 1.2
parents /ˈpeərənts/ 3.2
park (n) /pɑːk/ 3.1
party /ˈpɑːti/ 10.1
pasta /ˈpæstə/ 6.2
path /ˈpɑːθ/ 7.SP
peanuts /ˈpiːnʌts/ 3.1
pen /pen/ 9.2
pencil case /ˈpentsl keɪs/ 3.1

penguin /ˈpeŋgwɪn/ 11.2
people /ˈpiːpl/ CW3
pepper /ˈpepə/ 7.2
perfect (adj) /ˈpɜːfɪkt/ 2.2
perhaps /pəˈhæps/ 5.SP
person /ˈpɜːsn/ 4.1
personality /ˌpɜːsəˈnæləti/ 4.2
phone (n and v) /fəʊn/ 3.SP
photo /ˈfəʊtəʊ/ 2.2
photographer /fəˈtɒgrəfə/ 9.2
piano /piˈænəʊ/ 5.1
picture /ˈpɪktʃə/ 4.SP
piece /piːs/ 7.SP
(the) Pilgrim Fathers /ˈpɪlgrɪm ˈfɑːðəz/ 12.2
pillow /ˈpɪləʊ/ 5.2
pilot /ˈpaɪlət/ 11.3
place /pleɪs/ 3.2
plane /pleɪn/ 8.1
plastic /ˈplæstɪk/ 10.2
play (a sport/game) /pleɪ/ 5.1
play (the piano) /pleɪ/ 5.1
please /pliːz/ 1.2
Pleased to meet you. 3.3
pocket /ˈpɒkɪt/ 3.1
poem /ˈpəʊɪm/ 8.3
polite /pəˈlaɪt/ 8.3
pop concert /pɒp ˈkɒnsət/ 12.1
popular /ˈpɒpjələ/ 6.2
postcard /ˈpəʊstkɑːd/ 10.2
poster /ˈpəʊstə/ 7.2
potion /ˈpəʊʃn/ 4.2
power /paʊə/ 5.SP
practice /ˈpræktɪs/ 2.1
prefer /prɪˈfɜː/ 5.1
present /ˈprezənt/ CW2
president /ˈprezɪdənt/ 7.1
price /praɪs/ 12.3
primary school /ˈpraɪməri skuːl/ 11.3
prize /praɪz/ CW6
probably /ˈprɒbəbli/ 8.1
(radio/TV) programme /ˈprəʊgræm/ 2.3
progress /ˈprəʊgres/ 7.SP
pronounce /prəˈnaʊnts/ 8.1
pull /pʊl/ 9.SP
put /pʊt/ 5.1

Q

quarter /kwɔːtə/ 6.3
queen /kwiːn/ 7.SP
quiet /kwaɪət/ 4.1
(Be) Quiet! /kwaɪət/ 3.1
quite /kwaɪt/ 2.2

R

radio /ˈreɪdiəʊ/ 7.2

rain (n) /reɪn/ 12.1
rain (v) /reɪn/ 10.3
raincoat /'reɪnkəʊt/ 9.3
rat /ræt/ 5.2
read /riːd/ 5.1
reader /'riːdə/ 4.1
reading /'riːdɪŋ/ 2.2
ready /'redi/ 2.3
really /'rɪəli/ 4.1
recipe /'resɪpi/ 4.1
red /red/ 4.1
remember /rɪ'membə/ 2.1
resolution(s) /ˌrezə'luːʃn/ 10.2
restaurant /'restrɒnt/ 11.2
rich /rɪtʃ/ 12.SP
ride (a horse/bike) /raɪd/ 6.SP
riding /'raɪdɪŋ/ 3.SP
right (= correct) /raɪt/ 2.3
(on the) right /raɪt/ 7.3
ring (v) /rɪŋ/ 9.1
river /'rɪvə/ 2.3
road /rəʊd/ 1.2
room /ruːm/ 2.1
rubber /'rʌbə/ 1.3
rude /ruːd/ 8.3
rug /rʌg/ 7.3
ruler /'ruːlə/ 1.3
run /rʌn/ 9.2

S

sad /sæd/ 4.1
salad /'sæləd/ 6.2
same /seɪm/ 4.1
sandals /'sændlz/ 9.3
sandwich /'sænwɪdʒ/ 3.2
sardine /sɑː'diːn/ 7.2
sausage /'sɒsɪdʒ/ 6.2
save (someone) /seɪv/ 12.SP
save (money) /seɪv/ 11.2
say /seɪ/ 1.2
scared (of) /skeəd/ 4.2
scarf /skɑːf/ 9.1
school /skuːl/ 2.1
science /saɪənts/ 2.2
scientist /'saɪəntɪst/ 4.2
score (n) /skɔː/ 9.1
screen /skriːn/ 8.SP
sea /siː/ 1.1
seat /siːt/ 6.2
second /'sekənd/ 12.1
See you tomorrow. 1.3
send /send/ 8.SP
separate (v) /'sepəreɪt/ CW6
serious /'sɪəriəs/ 4.1
shark /ʃɑːk/ 5.2
shelf (pl shelves) /ʃelf/ 7.3
ship /ʃɪp/ 12.2
shirt /ʃɜːt/ CW5
shoe /ʃuː/ 9.2

shop (n) /ʃɒp/ 3.1
shopping /'ʃɒpɪŋ/ 7.2
shopping centre /'ʃɒpɪŋ
    'sentə/ 8.2
shopping list /'ʃɒpɪŋ lɪst/ 7.2
short /ʃɔːt/ 4.2
shorts /ʃɔːts/ 9.3
shout /ʃaʊt/ 9.2
(to have a) shower /ʃaʊə/ 6.3
side /saɪd/ 11.SP
sign /saɪn/ 3.SP
silent /saɪlənt/ 3.SP
silly /'sɪli/ 8.3
silver /'sɪlvə/ 4.1
sing /sɪŋ/ 8.1
singer /'sɪŋə/ 2.1
sister /'sɪstə/ 1.2
sit /sɪt/ 9.1
sit down /sɪt daʊn/ 7.2
skateboard /'skeɪtbɔːd/ 3.1
ski (v) /skiː/ 8.1
skirt /skɜːt/ 9.3
sky surfing /skaɪ 'sɜːfɪŋ/ 4.1
sleep /sliːp/ 6.1
small /smɔːl/ 4.1
smile /smaɪl/ 9.2
snack /snæk/ 6.2
snake /sneɪk/ 6.1
snow (v) /snəʊ/ 10.3
sock /sɒk/ 3.1
something /'sʌmθɪŋ/ 7.SP
sometimes /'sʌmtaɪmz/ 6.1
son /sʌn/ 3.3
soon /suːn/ 3.SP
Sorry! /'sɒri/ 1.3
(I'm) sorry /'sɒri/ 1.3
sound (n) /saʊnd/ 4.1
south /saʊθ/ 1.2
space /speɪs/ 11.1
spaceship /'speɪsʃɪp/ 11.1
spaghetti /spə'geti/ 6.2
speak /spiːk/ 5.1
special /'speʃl/ 5.SP
spell /spel/ 1.3
spider /'spaɪdə/ 5.2
sport /spɔːt/ 1.1
sports centre
    /spɔːts 'sentə/ 8.2
stadium /'steɪdiəm/ 9.3
stairs /steəz/ 3.2
stamp (v) /stæmp/ 2.3
stand /stænd/ 8.1
(pop) star /stɑː/ CW2
start (v) /stɑːt/ 11.3
(railway) station /'steɪʃn/ 8.2
stay /steɪ/ 10.1
steak /steɪk/ 5.1
(I've got a) stomach ache
    /'stʌmək eɪk/ 4.3

stone /stəʊn/ 4.SP
stop /stɒp/ 11.SP
story /'stɔːri/ 4.SP
straight /streɪt/ 4.2
strange /streɪndʒ/ 3.SP
street /striːt/ 8.2
strong /strɒŋ/ 9.SP
student /'stjuːdənt/ 2.1
study /'stʌdi/ 11.2
subject /'sʌbdʒɪkt/ 2.1
suddenly /'sʌdənli/ 6.SP
sunglasses /'sʌnˌglɑːsɪz/ 9.3
sunny /'sʌni/ 4.1
supermarket
    /'suːpəˌmɑːkɪt/ 7.2
support (a team) /sə'pɔːt/ 9.1
Sure. /ʃɔː/ 1.3
surf (the Net) /sɜːf/ 8.2
surfboard /'sɜːfbɔːd/ 4.1
surfing /'sɜːfɪŋ/ 2.2
surname /'sɜːneɪm/ 3.2
survey /'sɜːveɪ/ 2.2
survive /sə'vaɪv/ 12.2
sweater /'swetə/ 9.3
swim /swɪm/ 8.1
swimming /'swɪmɪŋ/ 2.2
swimming-pool
    /'swɪmɪŋ puːl/ 6.3

T

table /'teɪbl/ 7.3
take (a photo) /teɪk/ 9.2
talk /tɔːk/ 4.1
tall /tɔːl/ 4.2
tarantula /tə'ræntjələ/ 6.1
tea /tiː/ 6.2
teach /tiːtʃ/ 11.2
teacher /'tiːtʃə/ 1.2
teenager /'tiːnˌeɪdʒə/ 5.1
teeth /tiːθ/ 12.1
telephone /'telɪfəʊn/ 3.2
television /'telɪvɪʒn/ 4.1
telly addict /'teli ˌædɪkt/ 6.1
tennis /'tenɪs/ 2.2
tennis court /'tenɪs kɔːt/ 7.1
tennis racket
    /'tenɪs ˌrækɪt/ 3.1
terrified /'terəfaɪd/ 5.2
test (n) /test/ 9.2
text message
    /tekst 'mesɪdʒ/ 3.SP
Thanks! /θæŋks/ 1.3
Thank you. /θæŋk juː/ 6.2
That's all. /ðæts ɔːl/ 6.2
That's OK. /ðæts əʊ'keɪ/ 1.3
theatre /'θɪətə/ 12.1
then /ðen/ 9.SP
there /ðeə/ 2.1
thing /θɪŋ/ 1.1

think /θɪŋk/ 1.3
(I'm) thirsty /'θɜːsti/ 10.1
thunder /'θʌndə/ 5.2
ticket /'tɪkɪt/ 11.2
tidy (v) /'taɪdi/ 6.1
tiger /'taɪgə/ 11.2
time /taɪm/ 2.1
timetable /taɪm'teɪbl/ CW3
time zone /taɪm zəʊn/ 9.1
tired /taɪəd/ 4.3
tissues /'tɪʃuːz/ 3.1
toast /təʊst/ 6.2
today /tə'deɪ/ 1.3
toilet /'tɔɪlət/ 7.1
tomato /tə'mɑːtəʊ/ 7.2
tomato ketchup /tə'mɑːtəʊ
    'ketʃʌp/ 5.1
tomorrow /tə'mɒrəʊ/ 1.3
tongue /tʌŋ/ 6.1
tonight /tə'naɪt/ 8.3
too (= also) /tuː/ 3.2
too (+ adj) /tuː/ 5.2
top /tɒp/ 9.3
tortoise /'tɔːtəs/ 1.2
touch /tʌtʃ/ 7.SP
tourist /'tʊərɪst/ 5.2
towards /tə'wɔːdz/ 9.2
tower /taʊəʳ/ 5.2
town /taʊn/ 5.2
town centre /taʊn 'sentə/ 6.2
traffic /'træfɪk/ 8.2
train /treɪn/ 8.2
train (v) /treɪn/ 6.3
trainers /'treɪnəz/ 3.1
translate /trænz'leɪt/ 8.1
travel /'trævl/ 11.2
tree /triː/ 5.SP
tremble /trembl/ 5.2
trolley /'trɒli/ 7.2
trousers /'traʊzəz/ 9.3
true /truː/ 9.2
try /traɪ/ 1.2
T-shirt /'tiːʃɜːt/ 3.1
turn round /tɜːn raʊnd/ 11.SP
TV /ˌtiː'viː/ 3.1

U

UFO /ˌjuːef'əʊ/ 5.2
umbrella /ʌm'brelə/ 3.1
uncle /'ʌŋkl/ 3.3
under /'ʌndə/ 7.3
understand /ˌʌndə'stænd/ 1.1
uniform /'juːnɪfɔːm/ 5.1
university /ˌjuːnɪ'vɜːsəti/ 1.2
upstairs /ʌp'steəz/ 7.1
use (v) /juːz/ 1.2
useful /'juːsfl/ 3.1
usually /'juːʒəli/ 6.1

V

vampire /ˈvæmpaɪə/ 5.2
vegetables /ˈvedʒtəblz/ 5.1
vegetarian /ˌvedʒɪˈteəriən/ 5.1
very /ˈveri/ 2.2
video /ˈvɪdiəʊ/ 4.1
view /vjuː/ 8.2
visit /ˈvɪzɪt/ 5.2
voice /vɔɪs/ 8.SP
volcano /vɒlˈkeɪnəʊ/ 2.3
volleyball /ˈvɒlibɔːl/ 2.2

W

Wait a minute. 3.1
wait (for someone) /weɪt/ 10.SP
wake up /weɪk ʌp/ 8.2
walk (n) /wɔːk/ 5.2
walk (v) /wɔːk/ 5.2
wall /wɔːl/ 4.SP
want /wɒnt/ 2.2

wardrobe /ˈwɔːdrəʊb/ 7.3
wash /wɒʃ/ 8.3
watch (n) /wɒtʃ/ 3.1
watch (v) /wɒtʃ/ 3.1
water /ˈwɔːtə/ 6.1
wave /weɪv/ 9.2
way /weɪ/ 5.1
wear /weə/ 5.1
weather /ˈweðə/ 10.3
website /ˈwebsaɪt/ 8.1
week /wiːk/ 4.1
(at the) weekend
  /ˌwiːkˈend/ 6.1
Well done! /wel dʌn/ 2.3
well-organised /wel
  ˈɔːgənaɪzd/ 6.1
west /west/ 1.2
whale /weɪl/ 10.2
What a fantastic beach! 2.2
What about you? 1.2

What sort of ...? 5.3
What's it like? 4.1
What's the matter? 3.1
What's the time? 3.1
Where are they from? 2.1
Where do you come from? 5.3
wife /waɪf/ 3.3
wild /waɪld/ 11.2
win /wɪn/ CW6
wind /wɪnd/ 12.SP
window /ˈwɪndəʊ/ 1.3
windy /ˈwɪndi/ 10.3
wing /wɪŋ/ 8.1
winter /ˈwɪntə/ 12.2
with /wɪð/ 1.2
wizard /ˈwɪzəd/ 11.SP
woman /ˈwʊmən/ 4.SP
wood /wʊd/ 5.SP
work (n) /wɜːk/ 9.1
work (v) /wɜːk/ 9.SP

world /wɜːld/ 4.SP
write /raɪt/ 1.2
writer /ˈraɪtə/ 11.1
wrong /rɒŋ/ 2.3

Y

year /jɪə/ 5.2
Yes, please. /jes pliːz/ 2.3
yesterday /ˈjestədeɪ/ 12.1
yoghurt /ˈjɒgət/ 6.2
young /jʌŋ/ 12.2
Your turn. /jɔː tɜːn/ 4.2
You're welcome.
  /jɔː welkʌm/ 6.2

Z

zip /zɪp/ CW2
zoologist /zuˈɒlədʒɪst/ 11.2

Spelling notes

1 Word + -s

Look at what happens when we add -s to:

- words which end in
  -s, -sh, -ch, -x:

  a bus ➤ two buses
  a glass ➤ two glasses
  a fish ➤ two fishes
  a match ➤ two matches
  a box ➤ two boxes

  I guess ➤ he guesses
  I wash ➤ he washes
  I watch ➤ he watches
  I mix ➤ he mixes

- words which end in
  -o often add -es:

  a tomato ➤ two tomatoes
  a hero ➤ two heroes

  I go ➤ he goes
  I do ➤ he does

  BUT a radio ➤ two radios
    a piano ➤ two pianos
    a photo ➤ two photos

- words which end in
  consonant + -y:

  a family ➤ two families
  a balcony ➤ two balconies

  I try ➤ he tries
  I carry ➤ he carries

  BUT words which end
  in **vowel** + -y:
  a boy ➤ two boys
  a day ➤ two days

  I enjoy ➤ he enjoys
  I play ➤ he plays

- words which end in
  -f/-fe:

  a shelf ➤ two shelves
  a life ➤ two lives

2 Irregular plurals

Some nouns have an 'irregular' plural form.

a child ➤ two children
a person ➤ two people
a man ➤ two men
a woman ➤ two women

a foot ➤ two feet
a tooth ➤ two teeth

3 Word + -ing

Look at what happens when we add -ing to these verbs:

come ➤ coming
give ➤ giving

run ➤ running
sit ➤ sitting
swim ➤ swimming
travel ➤ travelling

4 Past simple + -ed

Look at the spelling of these verbs in the past simple:

live ➤ lived
love ➤ loved

stop ➤ stopped
travel ➤ travelled

carry ➤ carried
study ➤ studied

Lexical sets

Numbers

1 one
2 two
3 three
4 four
5 five
6 six
7 seven
8 eight
9 nine
10 ten
11 eleven
12 twelve
13 thirteen
14 fourteen
15 fifteen
16 sixteen
17 seventeen
18 eighteen
19 nineteen
20 twenty

21 twenty-one
22 twenty-two

30 thirty
31 thirty-one

40 forty
50 fifty
60 sixty
70 seventy
80 eighty
90 ninety

100 a hundred
101 a hundred and one
102 a hundred and two

200 two hundred
300 three hundred

1,000 a thousand
1,001 a thousand and one
1,100 one thousand one
    hundred

1,000,000 a million

Dates

1st first
2nd second
3rd third
4th fourth
5th fifth
6th sixth
7th seventh
8th eighth
9th ninth
10th tenth
11th eleventh
12th twelfth
13th thirteenth
14th fourteenth
15th fifteenth
16th sixteenth
17th seventeenth
18th eighteenth
19th nineteenth
20th twentieth
21st twenty-first
22nd twenty-second
30th thirtieth
31st thirty-first

Days of the week

Monday
Tuesday
Wednesday
Thursday
Friday
Saturday
Sunday

Months of the year

January
February
March
April
May
June
July
August
September
October
November
December

Countries and nationalities

Argentina	Argentinian
Australia	Australian
Austria	Austrian
Brazil	Brazilian
Britain	British
Canada	Canadian
China	Chinese
Colombia	Colombian
England	English
France	French
Germany	German
Greece	Greek
Holland	Dutch
India	Indian
Italy	Italian
Jamaica	Jamaican
Japan	Japanese
Mexico	Mexican
Morocco	Moroccan
New Zealand	New Zealander
South Africa	South African
Spain	Spanish
Sweden	Swedish
Turkey	Turkish
UK	British
USA	American

Irregular verbs

Basic form	Past simple
begin	began
buy	bought
come	came
do	did
drink	drank
eat	ate
fly	flew
go	went
get	got
get up	got up
have/have got	had
know	knew
leave	left
make	made
meet	met
put	put
read	read
see	saw
speak	spoke
wake up	woke up
wear	wore
write	wrote

Songs

Unit 1 Message In A Bottle

Look! – Where?
Look over there.
Look! – Where?
Look over there.

What is it? What is it?
It's a bottle, a bottle in the sea.
What's in it? What's in it?
In the bottle, the bottle in the sea?

Chorus:
It's a message.
It's a message for you.
It's a message.
It's a message for you.
It's a message in a bottle.
It's a message in a bottle.
It's a message in a bottle in the sea.

It's in English.
It's in English.
Do you understand?
What does it mean?

Chorus

Look! – Where?
Look over there.
Look! – Where?
Look over there.

Unit 4 The So Sad Blues

I've got red eyes.
My face is white.
I've got a heavy heart tonight.
You've got a one-way ticket on
    an aeroplane.
I've got the no, don't go, I'm so
    sad blues again.

The day is black.
My mood is blue.
My arms are empty.
I haven't got you.
You've got a one-way ticket on
    an aeroplane.
I've got the no, don't go, I'm so
    sad blues again.

I'm fed up.
I'm so sad.
This heartache is really bad.
You've got a one-way ticket on
    an aeroplane.
I've got the no, don't go, I'm so
    sad blues again.

Unit 5 Scared!

Are you scared of spiders?
Are you scared of sharks?
Do you start to tremble
When you're in the dark?
Do you believe in aliens
And UFOs?
Do you hide under your pillow
Late at night?

Chorus:
Are you scared?   Who? Me?
Are you scared?   No, I'm not.
(Repeat)
Yes, you are.   You're scared!
(Repeat x2)

Are you scared of thunder?
Are you scared of bats?
Do you start to tremble
When you think of rats?
Do you believe in vampires?
Do you believe in ghosts?
Do you hide under your pillow
Late at night?

Chorus

Unit 8 I Can't Dance

I can swim and I can dive.
I can stand on my head.
I can ride a bike.
I can. Oh yes I can!

I can cook and I can ski.
I can ride a horse.
I can speak Chinese.
I can. Oh yes I can!

Chorus:
But there's one thing that
    I can't do.
When the music starts, my legs
    don't move. Hey!
I can't dance. I can't dance. No, no!
(Repeat x3)

I can sing and I can draw.
I can play the guitar.
I can play football.
I can. Oh yes I can!

Chorus

Unit 10 Leaving

I'm going to catch a train.
I'm going to find a better place.
I don't want to see another
    dinosaur or whale.
I'm going to leave this job.
I'm leaving tonight.

I'm going to be free.
I'm going to be me.
I don't want to see this museum
    again.
I'm going to leave this job.
I'm leaving tonight.

Unit 12 Australia

I finished school on Tuesday.
I booked my ticket on Wednesday.
I bought some clothes on Thursday.
I packed my bag on Friday.

Chorus:
Let's go, let's go
To the other side of the world.
Why don't you come with me
To Australia?

I'm flying to Sydney on Sunday.
I'm gonna* swim with the sharks
    on Monday.
I'm gonna have fun
In the surf and the sunshine.

Chorus x 2

* = *going to*